Witness Your Why

Evangelism for Every Church

By Jeremy W. Scott

For Nate, Julia, Jeff & Margaret

Table of Contents

Witness Your Why

Introduction

This book is about evangelism. I know many people have an issue with that word and what they assume it means. It has been co-opted by a small group who stand on street corners proclaiming a version of the good news that doesn't seem all that good. That version of evangelism is not what I am after here, as I'm certain it is not the one that Jesus and the earliest disciples practiced. We are not selling fire insurance. This isn't about convincing people to believe in some variety of hell so we can save them from it. If for no other reason, doing so would be completely ineffective in the communities most of us live in today.

However you happen to identify socially, denominationally, or politically, all Christians should care about evangelism. At its most basic level evangelism is about recognizing we have our faith in a God of love who wants that love experienced by us and shared with others. Can anyone look around the world as it is and not say it could do with a little more love? That is the challenge we undertake when we do evangelism. It is about constantly asking ourselves, how can we make God's love and grace real to those around us? How do we turn God's grace into something people can see, hear, touch, taste, or smell? How do we make an abstract concept a real experience for those we encounter? This is the task of evangelism.

My evangelism professor in seminary, Dr. Joon-Sik Park, often said, "Mission is evangelism, and evangelism is mission." Amen, brother. I couldn't agree more. In my experience most churches resonate with this idea. Yet most also struggle to live it out. We tend to more easily do the mission part, the part where we collect food for the hungry, clothing for naked, and money for the far-off missionary. But when it becomes time to relate these activities to our faith, we struggle. We tend to think our belief in a loving God will just come through these activities by osmosis. Unfortunately it won't. We also hide behind excuses about perceived barriers in our way. We may not be allowed to carpet bomb our local school with free Jesus T-shirts, but honestly that's fine. Evangelism isn't about force or coercion. It's not impersonal. It's about relationships! Nothing is stopping you from forming a relationship with a principal or teachers at the local school. Nothing is stopping you from becoming a student mentor or classroom volunteer.

Sometimes God's grace looks like helping struggling students with their math.

The other unhelpful mind-set is the idea that we have to wait for the other person to make the first move. I've heard this expressed many ways, but it generally is a variation of: if you live a good life, people will get curious and ask you about it. Experience says this rarely, if ever, happens. Evangelism isn't about just reacting when people come to us. It's not a passive thing. Evangelism is about forming new relationships, and nearly always those relationships start with an invitation. An invitation isn't valid if it can't be declined. We have to respect the right of people to say no to whatever we are offering. God is very invested in people's right to choose how they relate to God. At the same time, people can't make a choice if they are never offered one.

Evangelism is about love and invitation. So drive from you mind any idea of standing with signs on the street corner that condemn groups of people or individuals. That is not what we are doing. Instead think of the last friend you made. For some of us it might have been a long time ago; that's okay. How did you become friends with that person? Chances are you met them somewhere like work, school, or church. You started to exchange pleasantries when you saw each other. Small talk likely grew deeper over time. Eventually one of you invited the other to some kind of shared experience. Maybe it was a meal, a party, or a sporting event. Whatever it was, there was

—

a progression where you discovered general mutual interest in each other. Evangelism follows a similar pattern. We are working to build new relationships between people and our church communities, with the goal of ultimately connecting them to God.

Humans are built to be social animals. Some of us make friends more easily than others, but none of us lasts long totally alone. So evangelism is something everyone can do. Some may invite dozens when others invite only a few, and that's fine. But don't for a minute think this isn't for you.

This book is designed to be used by a team. It's okay if you are a church leader and you want to preview it yourself first. That's a good idea, in fact. But if you want to make a real impact, you will need a team of people committed to bringing a healthy expression of evangelism to your church, even if it is only three or four people.

Each chapter has two sections. First are some important thoughts to consider, which are rooted in the example of the early church we find in the New Testament. Second are practical exercises your team can do to put those thoughts into practice. The more you invest in the exercises, the better off you will be. All of this is informed by my work with several new church starts. New church starts are the Research and Development arm of the church, and the lessons they learned can be applied to most existing congregations.

A few years ago I had some shoulder issues and my doctor sent me to a physical therapist for some help. It took him about twenty minutes to show me the basic stretches and exercises that he believed would help me. I went away thinking this would be pretty easy. I was wrong. The exercises were not technically difficult but in the first week I didn't see much improvement, and they took a lot of time I'd rather have spent doing something else. It was frustrating and I was tempted to quit. Later I went back for a follow-up and as I entered the therapy room I noticed the sign over the door. It read, "Physical Therapy works if you do!" Apparently I was not the only one who felt like I did. If you came to this book hoping to learn the clever low-impact solution for reaching new people with God's good news, I fear you will be disappointed. I have not yet uncovered any such thing. Instead, what working with numerous local churches and new church starts has taught me is there is no substitute for practicing the solid fundamentals of evangelism. There may be clever practices you discover along with way that will make you more efficient or effective, but they will only help if you first have the basics down.

Yes, this will take time and a lot of faith on your part. Faith in a loving God who is still blessing people. Faith that your church can join in the work God is up to in your community. Faith that you as leaders can equip and inspire others to be part of God's work. The good news is that our scriptures are full of stories of God using the most unlikely people to do exactly that. Do not assume for a minute that your church is too small, too old, too anything for God to do something

—

5

with. Whatever you come up with as an excuse, there is a story in scripture to show you different.

We have been given the great privilege of investing our time doing something quite amazing: telling people that God loves them. What can be better than that!

1. Can I Get a Witness?

One Sunday in the Spring of 2002, I wandered into Central United Methodist Church in Albuquerque, New Mexico for the early worship service after several years of not attending church. Nobody invited me, I knew nobody, and I sat by myself. I'm not sure what I thought I would find there, but a Methodist church had been part of my growing up and it just felt like the place to be. Over the weeks, months, and years that followed, I would get more involved with that congregation and eventually find myself changing careers, leaving software development, and heading into pastoral ministry.

There are many stories of those who have wandered away from the organized religion of their youth only to wander back later in life. Sometimes it's after college, or when they get married, or when the first kid comes. Some watershed moments in life seem to tip people back to the familiar places and communities of their past. In truth we, in the church, know this phenomenon well. We have counted on it for decades.

Stories like mine get repeated so often you would think it was a basic law of nature: "When our young people have kids, they'll be back." Believing this, the church continues to wait, passively, ready to receive back the sheep who have wandered away, the ninety-nine abdicating any responsibility to the one sheep who went missing. Instead we find it sufficient to have colorful brochures at the welcome table waiting for them whenever they happen to come home. The truth we don't want to face is that I am an endangered species. There are fewer and fewer people who have left organized religion who will ever return. Most who have wandered away will continue to ignore the church through marriage, children, divorce, and retirement. And if we are honest, many churches will continue to ignore them.

Those now called the "dones" have forever closed those chapters in their lives. The dones will not be lured back with contemporary music, smoothie bars, or skinny jeans. They barely notice our church buildings when they drive by and never read our clever signs. They don't care what color the carpet is or if you take communion monthly or weekly. I don't mean to sound harsh, but it is true. I also don't mean to dismiss having quality worship music, and I love a good smoothie as much as the next person. What I am saying is that if we expect people to just show up because we've made small changes to our worship, Sunday school, or whatever, we will be waiting a long time. The dones are truly done and it will take more intentional effort than most congregations are currently doing to reach them.

While the dones are a significant group in the American religious landscape today, they are by no means the fastest growing. That honor belongs to the "nones." While the dones may still call themselves nominally Christians, the nones claim, well, nothing. They are not accurately called atheists or even agnostics. Instead they have opted out of the whole conversation about religion. Most often, nones were raised with no religion and likely very little talk of faith in their homes. They are the children of the first wave of dones and don't know who Peter, Paul, Moses, or Noah are. They may know the name Jesus but have no more connection to it than they do Buddha or Muhammad.

Nones are one of the largest segments of the population in the US (23% in 2015)[1] and the fastest growing. They present a challenge to churches and denominations that still have an expectation that most people are raised with a basic understanding of what Christianity is and what churches do. Nones are blank slates when it comes to religion and pay no more attention to our churches than I, as a cisgender male, pay attention to women's shoe stores. They are not

---

[1]See http://www.pewresearch.org/topics/religiously-unaffiliated.

against us; they simply never think about us.

A few years ago, as a temporary transplant to Ohio, I always got myself in trouble in late November during the Ohio State vs. Michigan game. Not because I was a Michigan fan; I think that would have been more palatable. Instead, I was completely indifferent to the whole thing. Being indifferent and living in Columbus, the heart of Buckeye country, was an issue. Each year a noble few would try to indoctrinate me into the cause of the scarlet and gray by discussing the storied history of the rivalry, but I was often left asking the most basic of questions, like, what is a buckeye? The church finds itself in largely the same place. Our outreach practices and language all anticipate a certain level of church literacy that no longer exists. We must learn not only new skills but a new way of thinking about ourselves and, most importantly, why we do what we do.

I feel like I know a bit about the nones because, for several years now, I've been married to one. Those years I was slowly returning to church through the early morning service at Central UMC, she was home sleeping in. In fact, she liked that I went to church because it let her sleep in more. She was never against me going nor did she ask me many questions about it. She was happy to see it as that thing I did. Sure, we'd talk about God and faith from time to time, but, like many nones, she felt she had a handle on her own basic form of spirituality and felt no real draw to anything additional, least of all something that got in the way of sleeping in on the weekends.

Nones and dones aren't bad people, and for the most part they don't feel like they are missing out on much by not being part of a religious community. So for us, on the inside of churches we love, we have a big task in front of us. Evangelism today cannot take the form it did before. It is no longer about demonstrating that you have a better Sunday school than the church down the block, and we can no longer expect a gifted preacher to pack the pews. It simply won't work. Further, this isn't an excuse to slack off when it comes to worship or other discipleship practices in your church. They still have to be done at a high level of quality to continue to deepen the discipleship of those who are there. We all, through God's grace, are called to deepen our commitment to live in the ways Jesus demonstrated.

All of this can feel very discouraging. I totally understand that. It can also feel impossible. I understand that, too. But here is the good news: It doesn't have to. When done right, jumping into the work of modern evangelism is life giving, not draining. The Holy Spirit moves when we choose to go on an adventure for God and that feels amazing to be a part of. We also have a very good guide to help us with our impossible-feeling task. The earliest church lived in a time more similar to now than the environment the church lived in for most of the twentieth century. Those early followers were surrounded by indifferent people who had no clue who Jesus was. This can be our guide. Let's look at a couple of stories to show you what I mean.

Luke 10:1-11,17-20

After this the Lord appointed seventy others and sent them on ahead of him in pairs to every town and place where he himself intended to go. He said to them, "The harvest is plentiful, but the laborers are few; therefore ask the Lord of the harvest to send out laborers into his harvest. Go on your way. See, I am sending you out like lambs into the midst of wolves. Carry no purse, no bag, no sandals; and greet no one on the road. Whatever house you enter, first say, 'Peace to this house!' And if anyone is there who shares in peace, your peace will rest on that person; but if not, it will return to you. Remain in the same house, eating and drinking whatever they provide, for the laborer deserves to be paid. Do not move about from house to house. Whenever you enter a town and its people welcome you, eat what is set before you; cure the sick who are there, and say to them, 'The kingdom of God has come near to you.' But whenever you enter a town and they do not welcome you, go out into its streets and say, 'Even the dust of your town that clings to our feet, we wipe off in protest against you. Yet know this: the kingdom of God has come near.'"

The seventy returned with joy, saying, "Lord, in your name even the demons submit to us!" He said to them, "I watched Satan fall from heaven like a flash of lightning. See, I have given you authority to tread on snakes and scorpions, and over all the power of the enemy; and nothing will hurt you. Nevertheless, do not rejoice at this, that the spirits submit to you, but rejoice that your names are written in heaven."

This story happens during the ministry of Jesus, which is remarkable. Much of what we associate as the most powerful parts of his ministry haven't happened yet, obviously including his death and resurrection. In addition, many of the followers sent out in this passage had only just become aware of Jesus and who he was. These folks were not raised in Sunday school and taught to name the books of the Bible. They couldn't have; none of the New Testament had been written! Jesus sends out these very new followers with a general message of "God's kingdom coming near" and that's about it. Too often we fall into the trap that evangelism must lead with a deep theological understanding of God's grace or our understanding of Christ's atonement for our sins. But why? Not to say these things are not important, but it is a poor starting place that kills conversation before it can even start.

Those first followers of Jesus we find in Luke's writing brought a personal and relevant message into communities that had never heard of Jesus. We today, with our modern sensibilities, may scoff at the language of demons and Satan falling from heaven, but we should be careful not to judge too harshly a cultural context none of us has experienced. In a time before modern medicine, people still got sick and struggled with mental health issues just like today. These communities had no frame of reference for these things but the supernatural. So we must have some grace for our first-century counterparts. We also must look under the surface of the celebration found in this passage to understand it. What they are really celebrating is that they were able to make a real and positive impact on people by stepping out on faith, trusting God, and building relationships with new people in new places.

Our primary challenge now is to reclaim our faith in God's ability to touch and transform lives through us as followers of Jesus. There's still plenty of hurt and pain in the world and thus plenty of work for God to do. I doubt many people in our pews on Sunday morning have had the opportunity to witness the kind of healing in others these first followers did. Not because it is no longer possible, but because we rarely put ourselves in the position to be part of it. Those early followers weren't allowed to take so much as a change of clothes or spending money, yet we struggle to even speak about God outside our safe and comfortable church buildings.

This story should be powerfully convicting to anyone who takes the Christian faith seriously. As followers of Christ we can't ignore the call he puts on us to be proclaim "the kingdom of God is near." Meaning, God's love is around us, available to all, and inviting all into a transformational experience. As the cliché goes, God loves you just the way you are, and God loves you too much to leave you that way. So true. But if we aren't willing to step out and do the things necessary to bring that message to the wider world, who is going to do it?

This first followers had their eyes open to something we must never forget. They were successful in new places and among new people because God was already at work in those communities. They might have been introducing people to the name of Jesus, but what they were really doing was providing a proper noun to something already at work. Part of being a Christian is to believe that God is at work in the world, the entire world, even in places ignorant of, or indifferent to, the Christian faith. It is not our job to bring God to people. The Holy Spirit is already there. It is our job to see where God is already working and join in that work. We should not be afraid of evangelism because God is already doing the hardest part. Our job is to simply join in.

Acts 1:4-9

While staying with them, he ordered them not to leave Jerusalem, but to wait there for the promise of the Father. "This," he said, "is what you have heard from me; for John baptized with water, but you will be baptized with the Holy Spirit not many days from now."

So when they had come together, they asked him, "Lord, is this the time when you will restore the kingdom to Israel?" He replied, "It is not for you to know the times or periods that the Father has set by his own authority. But you will receive power when the Holy Spirit has come upon you; and you will be my witnesses in Jerusalem, in all Judea and Samaria, and to the ends of the earth." When he had said this, as they were watching, he was lifted up, and a cloud took him out of their sight.

This passage obviously comes from the very end of Jesus' ministry on earth. He is giving his final instructions to the disciples and is turning over the ministry he began to them. From this point on people would have the responsibility to share the message that Jesus had shared for the last three years. Many point to the next chapter and the coming of the Holy Spirit in the upper room as the birth of the church. But for me, this part is equally as important because this is where we find our purpose: we are to be *witnesses*.

What starts this exchange is a question from an unnamed disciple, asking about the restoring of the kingdom of Israel. This is important because, while the Jews may be living in Israel and worshiping in the temple in Jerusalem, they are not actually in charge of their own land. They have been conquered by the Romans, who remind them constantly with shows of military force that they are a subservient people. Most people in this time when they thought about a messiah would think about Moses. What they are looking for in a new messiah is a modern Moses with a bit of a twist. They didn't want to be led out of Israel the way the original Moses led them out of Egypt. Instead, they want a new Moses who would force the Romans out of the land they were already living in. They were looking for a political change and Jesus refuses to commit to that. Instead he gives them a different mission altogether: They will be witnesses.

I believe Jesus chose his words here carefully. A witness is someone who has seen or experienced something and then relates the experience to others.

To be a witness you must have both parts. Someone who experiences something but does not share about it is simply a participant. Those who share with others something they did not personally see or experience is at best a storyteller and at worst a liar. To be a witness we must first become skilled at seeing and experiencing where God is at work. For the first disciples, fresh off three years following Jesus around, this is pretty straightforward. While it may not feel as straightforward today, we cannot believe it is impossible. If God is still at work in our lives, our churches, and our communities, surely as people of faith we are seeing and experiencing it, right?

In my experience, when even longtime church participants are asked to be witnesses they struggle first with coming up with experiences to share. Not because they don't have them, but because they are inexperienced at recognizing them. This is the first skill we must learn. Let me tell you a short story to illustrate the point.

I served a declining, just-off-downtown church as my first appointment out of seminary. In my second year there a small group of people decided they wanted to do something to bless the neighborhood, so they opened a free store that focused on clothing and household items in some unused Sunday school rooms. This was a place where anyone could come and take what they needed, no questions asked. A few months in, I was milling around when I observed something interesting but not uncommon. A mother was in the waiting area, sharing with a volunteer. She was a single mother with a son who was well over six feet tall. He had been invited to a statewide choir event but needed some black dress pants to attend, which were proving very difficult to find at a reasonable price. She had never been to the free store before but driving by she thought she would just give it a try. The volunteer heard her story and headed upstairs to the sorting room to see what she could find.

In the upstairs room were over a dozen boxes labeled "men's pants," and she started digging. Somewhere in the bottom of box five or six, she came across a stash of pants that must have been previously owned by an NBA player. They were well within the size range she was looking for, so she grabbed the stack and headed back to the waiting room. There she found the mother and handed her the stack that included two pairs of black pants, a few pairs of like-new jeans, and a few random other pairs. As I looked through the door I saw our guest and the deep look of surprise she had on her face. And then the tears came from both the mother and the volunteer.

When you encounter stories like this you have a choice in how you see them. You can see it as simply happenstance or the free store doing what it was designed to do. Or, you can choose to see the Holy Spirit moving all around it. I choose the latter. I choose to see the Holy Spirit working through the volunteer who invested time in hearing the story of the single mom. I also see the Holy Spirit moving in the mother in her willingness to make herself vulnerable and share her struggles with a stranger. I see the Holy Spirit inspiring a church to open its doors in a new way and to recognize the abundance in the community around them and organize that abundance.

I find our greatest challenge is not that God isn't moving in our communities but that we fail to see it. Pastors and other leaders have not done a good job training their folks to recognize the signs of God's work. In truth, we seem to have pretty low expectations of God in our daily lives. That will not serve us well. To be the witnesses Jesus challenges us to be we must first recognize when we are seeing and experiencing God's handiwork.

So take a minute and think through the last few days. It may not be as exciting as pants (ha!), but is there a place God showed up? How did God work through you to be a blessing to you or others? What is coming to mind may seem small and that's fine. God does not part the Red Sea often. And don't forget the person God might be trying to reach is you! I find it altogether too common that church people are quick to help others and slow to ask for and receive the help they need.

So the first part of being a witness is to see and experience God at work. The second part is to share the experience with others. While our skill at the first part may be atrophied, the second part tends to scare us to death. This is a fear we must conquer, and soon. Sharing Jesus is not about standing on street corners shouting into microphones or handing out cards with clever sayings. These are unhelpful and ineffective strategies. Instead, sharing in the way Jesus intends is about cultivating relationships. Real relationships, that are about mutual respect and not weighed down by ulterior motives.

A fundamental belief in the Christian tradition is that we follow a God who loves all of us. All of us. ALL OF US. Nobody is excluded. And this love is the thing we are witnesses to. Our motivation to share with others is to share this love. We do this because we recognize a life lived with more love is better than one lived with less. In the end, this is not about growing our church to have more people to serve on committees and put money in the plate. That may happen, but it's not the primary aim. People will know immediately if you have the wrong motives.

The rest of this book will show you how to build a relationship-cultivating system in your church. This does not mean everyone will become your best friend, but if you want to reach new people with God's love, somebody in your faith community needs to know their name. Names, as it turns out, are very important. One of the first things I learned about the Bible in seminary was to pay attention to people who are named because it signals they are an important character in the story. We cherish people's names because we want people to feel important and because we know they are important to God.

Get to Work

Learning to see God at work in your life, church, and community is critical. This can only be learned through practice. Sometimes God in our lives comes in the form of unexpected blessings. Sometimes it's about having our eyes opened to a new experience or truth. And sometimes, quite simply, it breaks our heart. Sometimes the work God needs to do is to wake us up to the injustice happening around us.

Reflect back over the last week or so and ask yourself the following questions:

1.   Where were you blessed?
2.   Where did you learn something new?
3.   Where was your heart broken?

Then ponder what God might be trying to tell you through these experiences.

Teamwork

As a team, think about your church. God acts on us as individuals and as groups. For your church community, ask yourself the following questions:

1.   Where has your church been blessed?
2.   Where has your church blessed others?
3.   Where has your church encountered something new?

Then discuss together what God might be trying to tell you.

Finally, as a team, think about the community around you. God is at work in your community even among those who do not know who God is. For the community around your church, ask yourself the following questions:

1. Where is your community in pain?
2. Where is your community being blessed?
3. Who or what is new in your community?

Then discuss together what God might be trying to tell you.

People will learn to see God at work most effectively when it is modeled for them. The ancient practice of testimony is an amazing tool to teach with. As you cultivate stories of God's work in your personal life, the life of your church, and the life of your community, what are three places you could share those stories:

1. _____

2. _____

3. _____

Some churches make testimony part of worship during Lent, Advent, or special sermon series. Others may do it at church-wide events, recorded on Facebook, or in the newsletter. The key to success with any testimony is to make sure that people prepare. You don't want folks winging it in front of the congregation on Sunday morning. Have people write down what they are going to say and make sure it is reviewed ahead of time. With that caveat, some practice of regular testimony can be transformational for any church. It allows people to see what being a witness truly is and the inspirational effect it can have. To be witnesses we must, well, be witnesses.

Can I get a witness!?

2. Know Your Why

Congregations will need to do new things to reach new people, that is sure. There is no getting around it if we are going to be the witnesses God calls us to be. But the first step is not to start a bunch of random programs. That will just chew through your time and resources. The first thing we need to do is take a good look at what we are already doing and ask ourselves *why* we are doing it. We won't get anywhere without knowing that first.

Some congregations don't really know why they do the things they do, beyond habit and tradition. Or, if they do think about it in more missional or spiritual terms it tends to be a bit shallow and inwardly focused. Please don't take this as a blanket criticism of all churches. Tradition has served us well for many years. We do the things we do for a reason, and that reason often is that, at one time, it worked for us. Today, we have a different set of challenges and opportunities, so our inherited ways of being church won't serve us as well as they did. That is why we need to reconsider *why* we do what we do as a first step in rethinking what we do and how we do it.

For example, think about the current worship experience in your church. Why do you do it the way you do it? Take a minute and ponder that question then continue.

Some people will say something like, "We do it the way we always have done it." That may be true, but it's not really an answer to why. Some might go a little further and say, "We do it this way because it's familiar and comfortable for people." Again, that may be true, but is that a good why? Do we do things just because they are comfortable? Finally, there are some who will say something like, "We worship the way we do because it allows us to experience God's love." This is a better answer, but it is still lacking something.

For most people, worship is the defining act of the church. It is the one thing, above all things, that must be present for us to consider it *real* church. That is why it's critical for us to know our why of worship, because for most people the why of our worship is the why of church as a whole. If we don't have that one right then everything we do is at a disadvantage.

We will come back to worship in a bit, but first I want to demonstrate the importance of knowing your why using an example most people have heard of: Netflix. Netflix has become a media juggernaut, creating top-tier entertainment and quickly becoming the way many people connect with movies and TV shows. We can now access amazing content, oftentimes made by Netflix itself, from a whole range of devices, including the phones we all carry with us all the time. Netflix has become so well known as the world's premiere streaming media service we forget that the company actually started as a different business, sending DVDs in the mail.

DVDs by mail is how I first encountered Netflix. My wife and I subscribed to the three-disk-a-month service and most months got through six or seven movies. We were excited when our disks started to arrive about a day earlier because Netflix had opened a new sorting center closer to our home. For a time, Netflix was opening new shipping and sorting centers all over the country very quickly. They had created an amazing proprietary system of hardware and software that let them sort and mail an unbelievable number of disks fast and inexpensively. When Blockbuster[2] finally tried to compete in DVD delivery, Netflix was so far ahead they didn't stand a chance.

Netflix became the most dominant DVD service in the world in only a few years. While that service continues to exist, it is not what most people know Netflix for now. Instead, we know them as creators of high-quality content that is delivered over the

---

[2] For the younger people out there, Blockbuster was a video store chain where you had to physically go to the store to rent movies. Ask your parents about it.

internet. Reed Hastings, the founder of Netflix, has spoken many times about their pivot away from DVD-by-mail toward streaming. What is most fascinating about that story is that the streaming platform was developed with the same engineers and designers who developed the DVD-by-mail system. After investing years in becoming the world's best and most efficient DVD handlers, they purposely slowed that development, closed sorting centers they'd invested millions of dollars in, and invested instead in a whole new technology to power the Netflix we know now.

Think about that. How difficult would it be to set aside something you have invested so much time and money into and start doing something very different? Would people feel all the blood, sweat, and tears they put into the first iteration of Netflix was a waste? How did they not feel overwhelmingly discouraged? The answer is simple: They knew their *why*.

Reed was very clear about the kind of culture he wanted to create at Netflix. He wanted people to be innovative, risk taking, and not afraid to fail. He also wanted people to be very clear about what they were doing and why they were doing it. Netflix has famously posted on its website a long description of the culture of the company that any new employee must review and agree to. That description begins with the statement:

> *We [Netflix] connect people with stories. Lots of people, and lots of stories. Our hundred million global members are a good start, but someday, we*

> *hope to entertain everyone. Entertainment, like
> friendship, is a core human need. No matter how
> big or small, dramatic or satiric, entertainment
> stimulates us, changes the way we feel, and gives
> us common ground.* [3]

This very clear articulation of their *why* is what has given Netflix the ability to pivot when they need to. They aren't in the DVD-by-mail business. They aren't even in the streaming media business. They are in the *connecting people with stories* business. They are in the *meeting a core human need* business. When it became clear that streaming was the future and DVDs were on their way out then, of course, they made the switch. What else could they do?

The counterexample is the one already mentioned: Blockbuster. Blockbuster was in the video store business and couldn't survive once people started connecting with movies at home in a new way. Blockbuster really didn't understand their why. They knew what they did (rent videos), and how they did it (through their stores), but they really didn't understand their why in the same way Netflix did. Which means they were left behind.

You should be seeing some similarities between Netflix, Blockbuster, and the church. There are many lessons for us to learn here. Netflix talks about its purpose not in terms of dollars or market share but in terms of basic human needs. They recognize that

---

[3] See https://jobs.netflix.com/culture/#introduction.

people across time and cultures have sought out entertainment. They are staying rooted in that and letting the *what* and *how* of their business shift. This is why churches really shouldn't spend a lot of time focused on weekly worship attendance numbers. It's not helpful because we are not in the *getting people to worship business*. Honestly, we're not. We are in the *connecting people to God* business!

No doubt Netflix kept track of the number of DVDs it was shipping. But what would have happened if that one number became the most critical metric in the company? Would they have moved to streaming? Likely not, because it wouldn't help DVD numbers.

Similarly, when we get hung up on things like worship attendance we can get fixated on the wrong thing. Our why is not to get people into worship. Our why is to connect people with the transformational power of God's love and grace. So back to the question we started with, what is the why of worship? It is not simply to get people to show up. A worship experience where many people show up but nobody connects with God in a new or deeper way is a failure. Conversely, a small group of people gathering for worship where people grow in their understanding and experience of God through the Holy Spirit is an unequivocal success!

Instead of asking, "How can we get more people to attend worship?" we should be asking, "How can we make worship more Spirit led? How can we give people a more robust experience of God's grace?"

And, "How can we invite new people into a new or deeper relationship with God through worship?" If we focus on these questions, we will find that things like worship attendance will likely take care of themselves with time.

Netflix has crafted a brilliant why and congregations should strive to create something similar. There are some attributes of the Netflix statement that should be in any why statement. First, it is focused on people, not activities. Netflix isn't in the movie business; it is in the people business, and so is the church. We are in the disciple-making business, which requires us to focus on people. So any valid church why should focus on people first and foremost.

Second, Netflix talks in terms of the basic human need for entertainment. Visit anybody anywhere, even those who have never seen a television, and you will find some form of entertainment. It may be singing songs, drumming, or the telling of stories. Whatever it is, humans have been entertaining themselves for as long as there have been humans to entertain. Your church why should tap a similar basic human need. If we truly believe all people are made in God's image then there must be some commonality between us. It may be the need for companionship, the ability to make a difference in the world, or a felt connection with a higher power. What needs is your church meeting for people? After all, God does not intend us to stay static. We are called to grow and evolve into better witnesses of God's love. Any church why must be focused on the development of people into the version of themselves that God most desires.

For many churches, if we are being very honest, their why may be something like, "We are loving and caring for people as they move from this life to the next." Let me say there really isn't anything wrong with this. This is a people-focused why based on a real need. However, if this is the why at your core it's easy to understand why younger people may not be quick to get involved. What if instead a church attempted to live out a why that was more like, "We help people move through all stages of life knowing God's love for them. We connect people with others so we can share our burdens and celebrations." Here our older members are still recognized and cared for and the struggles of being a young person or new parent are honored as well. Most importantly we honor the gifts various groups have to offer each other and the blessing diversity is to any community.

A real why statement, like in the Netflix example, exists somewhere between a tagline and a manifesto. A tagline is great for putting on shirts and stickers. At my last church our tagline was "Act Your Faith," which I still like. A manifesto is paragraphs if not pages and may touch on several philosophical and theological topics. They are often sectioned out on the "About Us" section of church websites. A why statement will be sentences, not paragraphs, and be to the point. Here is an example from Belong Church, a new church start in the Denver area:

Belong   is   a   Christian   community   that   values,

---

welcomes, and affirms the full diversity of all people…. [We are] a place where many people gather together and explore the many ways in which God has been moving in our lives. By joining together in an inclusive, justice oriented community, we have the opportunity to encourage each other, challenge ourselves, and transform our world through the radical and redemptive love of Jesus.[4]

Matthew 28:16-20

Now the eleven disciples went to Galilee, to the mountain to which Jesus had directed them. When they saw him, they worshipped him; but some doubted. And Jesus came and said to them, "All authority in heaven and on earth has been given to me. Go therefore and make disciples of all nations, baptizing them in the name of the Father and of the Son and of the Holy Spirit, and teaching them to obey everything that I have commanded you. And remember, I am with you always, to the end of the age."

This passage is often called the Great Commission. These are the final words of Jesus in Matthew's gospel and set a course for the church that would follow after Jesus' time on earth. It is clear from this passage that our function is to connect people with God above everything else. We do this because we believe a life lived in relationship with God, experiencing God's love and grace, is important. We believe that life is hard and often overwhelming, and our faith helps us

---

[4] https://www.belongchurch.org/about/who-we-are/

understand we are not alone, but that the creator of the universe is with us. This is a powerful and life-changing idea! Our task then is to act as if we really trust this idea and find in ourselves a desire to share it with others.

Desire plays a huge role in any evangelism effort. We need to want to share good news with others. This desire often comes from a place of personal experience. We first need to recognize that our connection with God is valuable to us before we can hope to show the value of it to others.

I've worked with dozens of congregations over the last several years. Many are looking for solutions to declining giving and participation in worship. Many want to get to work doing things as quickly as possible to grow their church. Most are then surprised when the first thing I require them to do is to spend two full months praying. Yes, two months. And it's not optional.

This kind of work requires a team of people to be successful. The pastor cannot be the only evangelist in the church. Ultimately every follower of Jesus has a calling to share the good news with others. That said, it is absurd to think you can get everyone going at once. You will need a team of brave souls willing to go first, experiment, and learn the new skills required. That team needs to be well connected to each other and to God.

Without fail some individuals in each church will resist this request. I've heard every reason you can think of why they can't or shouldn't do it. Most will point to the urgency they feel about their current situation and question spending that much time on prayer. They feel a pull to do something that feels more constructive or on point. Yet, for followers of Jesus, what could be more constructive than praying? The other thing that happens without fail is that, when all is said and done, people report that the most valuable part of our whole church vitality process is the time they spent in prayer with each other. Oftentimes it is the people who were the most resistant who end up being the most changed by the experience of regular spiritual practice.

If you are going to be successful in any form of evangelism you will need a team that is deeply connected to God. Every person in the group should be able to relate a recent and impactful movement of the Holy Spirit in their own lives. If they can't, then before you do anything further, it's imperative that you invest in the spiritual life of your team. These kinds of experiences are the fuel your team, and really your whole church, run on. You won't get far without them.

When I have churches take the two months to pray, their weekly gatherings are pretty simple and based on a longtime small group model. In my tradition, United Methodist, we call these Band meetings or Wesleyan Small Groups. The basic outline goes like this:

- Accountability Questions (How is it with your soul?)
- Spiritual Formation Activity

- Prayer Partners
- Closing Ritual

If our *why* is about helping people connect with the life-giving goodness of God then we need a team that is tapped into that same source. Then we are not just speaking from our intellectual understanding of faith but are also being informed by our own personal encounters.

As you can see by all of this, evangelism isn't actually about growing your church or finding more people to put money in the plate to support your budget. The why of church is first and foremost about relationships between people and God. We live in a world that is full of divisiveness. Things we thought we were leaving behind, like racism, sexism, and homophobia, now seem more present than ever. It is hard to know if we are seeing the last gasps of bygone evils or a resurgence of timeless human failings. Either way, our times cry out for voices who will speak for justice and reconciliation. This is hard and demanding work and, if we are going to be successful, we must hold fast to some basic truths. The most basic of which is that love and tolerance, not hate and vitriol, are at the foundation of all creation.

It is no wonder to me that the most renowned justice seekers of the last century were people of faith. People like Dorothy Day, Mahatma Gandhi, and Martin Luther King Jr. were all people of faith. Their faiths might have been different, but they all had a real connection to a God of love who propelled them forward into often dangerous places. We have plenty of people today who are navigating treacherous conditions like inner city violence, rural decay and the drug addiction that comes with it, or fighting for the right to publicly love who they feel called to love. We are in just as much need for a connection to the source of love and grace as at any time in the past.

Evangelism is not about winning people, keeping score, and telling others why they are wrong. We are instead witnesses to the source of hope that we all crave. Surely there are plenty who love justice and act with mercy who are not people of faith. There are some who are antagonistic to religion and those who choose to practice it. So be it. Our job is to know and claim the truth of our lives first and foremost. We live in world too full already with us and them; we do not need to create more.

Matthew 22:34-40

When the Pharisees heard that he had silenced the Sadducees, they gathered together, and one of them, a lawyer, asked him a question to test him. "Teacher, which commandment in the law is the greatest?" He said to him, "'You shall love the Lord your God with all your heart, and with all your soul, and with all your mind.' This is the greatest and first commandment. And a second is like it: 'You shall love your neighbor as yourself.' On these two commandments hang all the law and the prophets."

One of the most striking things about the story of Jesus we find in the Bible is that his harshest criticisms are always aimed at the religious leaders of his day. These leaders are part of the same religious tradition as Jesus. He rarely utters a word against those of other faiths, but instead directs his ire toward those from his own house who he feels should know better. Jesus has no time for those who would use their shared faith to justify self-serving agendas. There are many stories, like the one above, of him sparring with leaders and politicians of his day. In each of these matches his most powerful tool is to remind them of their shared why, like he does above.

Before the encounter in this passage several others try to trap Jesus by pointing out what they see as inconsistencies in what he is teaching. They argue nuance and detail with him, all of which Jesus answers deftly. When it is time to bring the whole encounter to a close, though, he changes tactics completely. He stops arguing point by point and brings it all to a much more fundamental place. Answering the question, "What is this whole faith about?" Jesus' reply is simple; it's about two things and two things only: loving God and loving neighbor.

Those who choose to engage in evangelism can find themselves in similar situations as Jesus often found himself in. Also like Jesus, we can end up in heated debates with others from the same household of faith as us. Christians differ dramatically on our interpretations of some parts of scripture and these differences have led to division and mistrust between us. I would be the last to say we should avoid theological debate. It is necessary to reach new places of understanding. But what we can never do, if we are to call ourselves true Christians, is to leave behind the call to love God and neighbor that Jesus himself put at the center of our faith.

One way we must learn to be more like Jesus is to learn that when things get heated we must first step out of the details of the disagreement and ask ourselves, are we showing love to our neighbor right now? Are we loving God? Or has something else crept into the exchange? Similarly, we must be prepared to hold our fellow followers of Jesus accountable to the standard Jesus set for us. We must be prepared to remind those who try to use judgement, bigotry, or intolerance to advocate for their version of Christianity they are simply doing it wrong. There is no place for those things in a religion founded to advocate for God's love of all people and the expectation that we all treat each other with love.

You cannot argue someone into faith by pointing out all the places they are falling short. You also can't argue another Christian onto your side of by parsing scripture down to the smallest degree. All you will accomplish with either tactic is to further entrench whoever it is you are talking to. Going down that path trades the most powerful part of our religious tradition for weak attempts to score points at the expense of someone else. If Netflix can build a billion-dollar empire on the basic human need for entertainment, surely the church can blossom in our world going after even more central longings: the longing for connection, acceptance, and love.

Know your why. Know why you do what you do and cling to it above all the pettiness you will no doubt encounter. Do that, keep yourself close to God, and as Paul writes in his letter to the Romans, "If God is for us, who can be against us?"

Get to Work

Go back and review the introductory statement from the Netflix culture document. Notice how it doesn't talk in terms of DVDs, streaming, or any other nuts and bolts of what Netflix does. It also doesn't use any insider corporate language. Instead, it's written in everyday, universal terms about basic human needs and is focused on people, not products. Reflect on this statement and start to draft one for your church.

- Brainstorm a list of the basic human needs your church attempts to meet.
- Remove any "churchy" words or phrases.[5]
- Begin to form 5-8 sentences that articulate the "why" of your church.
- Make sure it is people focused (not activities or products).

Avoid making your why too broad. Netflix is focused on one thing: entertainment. Congregations will likely be a little broader than that, but not too much. One reason new church starts are often better at reaching new people than existing churches is that they know their why. The know who they want to be. They be focused on issues of justice and confronting racism. They may be focused on families with young

---

[5] Even words like "Worship" are problematic to nones and dones. Some churches use "Celebration" instead. Also avoid: Sanctuary, Sunday School, Bible Study, or Narthex.

kids and the challenges they encounter. They may be focused on new retirees, those who care about the environment, or those seeking intimate community through dinner church. New church starts that start off trying to be all things to all people don't often survive. The same is true for existing churches.

What is your church's why? Why do you uniquely exist? What can God do through you that God can't do through anybody else?

Practice speaking your why aloud. Imagine someone asked you about your church and you wanted to share your why with them. You should be able to get it out in less than thirty seconds. Divide you team into pairs and practice, one person requesting, "Tell me about your church," and the other responding with your why.

Do not continue until you have a clear why. The rest of this book will do you no good without it.

You will want to revisit this as you continue in this book, but always keep it in front of you. Print it up on small cards and put it in your book, in your Bible, and tape it to the pulpit. As you continue you should be constantly asking yourself how what you're doing reflects your why. If it doesn't, ask yourself, should you really be doing it?

How can you share your why? Video, sermon series, or newsletter articles could be a start. You need to invite others to explore your church's why and give them a chance to buy in.

Three ways you will share your why

1. _____

2. _____

3. _____

3. The Gift of Translation

Acts 2:1-13

When the day of Pentecost had come, they were all together in one place. And suddenly from heaven there came a sound like the rush of a violent wind, and it filled the entire house where they were sitting. Divided tongues, as of fire, appeared among them, and a tongue rested on each of them. All of them were filled with the Holy Spirit and began to speak in other languages, as the Spirit gave them ability.

Now there were devout Jews from every nation under heaven living in Jerusalem. And at this sound the crowd gathered and was bewildered, because each one heard them speaking in the native language of each. Amazed and astonished, they asked, "Are not all these who are speaking Galileans? And how is it that we hear, each of us, in our own native language? Parthians, Medes, Elamites, and residents of Mesopotamia, Judea and Cappadocia, Pontus and Asia, Phrygia and Pamphylia, Egypt and the parts of

Libya belonging to Cyrene, and visitors from Rome, both Jews and proselytes, Cretans and Arabs—in our own languages we hear them speaking about God's deeds of power." All were amazed and perplexed, saying to one another, "What does this mean?" But others sneered and said, "They are filled with new wine."

The gift of the Holy Spirit Jesus promised in Acts chapter one shows up in the very next chapter. While Jesus will no longer be with the disciples in person, they are not alone. The Holy Spirit will now be their guide and enabler on their mission to be witnesses to God's work in the world. The Holy Spirit also doesn't waste any time getting to work.

Pentecost is not an exclusively Christian holiday. Its roots go deeper than that into Jewish practices common in the time of Jesus. Pentecost was a time of pilgrimage where faithful Jews from all over the Middle East would travel to Jerusalem for religious festivals. The timing was ripe to practice the craft of witnessing, but there was a challenge. Because people came from all over, they also came speaking many different languages. In this time it was not common for people to travel great distances or marry outside of their small villages. So there were many regional languages and dialects that developed in these isolated populations. And these populations did not interact with each other on a regular basis. In fact, there were far more variations in language then than you would encounter today.

If the story of Jesus is going to have a chance, it is

going to have to be translated into words and concepts that can be understood by diverse groups of people. So, the first gift of the Holy Spirit is one of translation. Suddenly, the disciples found themselves speaking languages we assume they did not previously know. We can struggle with stories like this in the Bible. Few of us expect to wake up one day and find ourselves fluent in a language we've never studied. It's just not a common occurrence. We know from the reaction of the crowd it wasn't a common thing at the time either. They are shocked and amazed to say the least. Some even assume the disciples are drunk! Then, as now, it seems being drunk early in the morning was not socially acceptable behavior.

It's worth taking a little aside here to note that the miracle we find in Acts 2 is not the same thing as speaking in tongues as it's practiced by Pentecostal and charismatic Christian communities. In those places, the language spoken is not an *earthy* language but a *spiritual* one. That is why scripture talks about the need of a translator for such situations. In this story, the disciples are speaking known oral languages of their day.

Spending time debating the plausibility of spontaneous language fluency misses the most important point this story is trying to teach. The scriptures are clear to point out that it is the disciples who are able to speak a new language and those in the crowd are hearing in their native tongues. The gift of translation is from the speaker, not the listener. Put another way, it is the disciples, the witnesses, who are doing the work of translation, not the uninitiated crowd. It is the job of the speaker to use a language people can understand, not the job of the crowd to learn the language the speaker wants to use.

Throughout the twentieth century and into the twenty-first, translating the Bible has been a big deal. While the major languages of the world have had Bible translations for centuries, smaller communities have been left out. It is still common to find groups of hundreds or thousands of people in isolated places whose first language is only oral. Many populations, especially more isolated tribes in places like South America, have never developed a written form of language simply because they have never needed one. Today that leads to problems, as it is harder and harder for isolated communities to avoid interacting with the wider world. Preservation of native language, culture, and customs requires a written language.

When Christian missionaries encountered these communities they faced two possible options when it came to sharing scripture. They could either try to teach these communities one of the languages the Bible already exists in, thus putting the burden on them. Or, they could take the time, learn their language, help them develop a written form, then translate the Bible into the native tongue people were already familiar with. Needless to say the second option takes far greater effort on the part of the missionaries and requires developing grammars and dictionaries before you can even begin translating anything else.

Today, hundreds of lesser-known languages have both written and oral forms because of the work of missionaries. It often takes the better part of a decade to complete a translation, and requires people to live with and learn all about the cultures of the communities they are trying to reach. It is a massive undertaking that still continues. Not only is it providing an opportunity to share God's love, it is also helping to preserve and protect isolated cultures and languages.

All this work has continued for decades outside the United States while, at the same time, many churches in the United States have become more and more indifferent to their neighborhoods, and less and less in tune with the culture of the people who surround them. If we are going to overcome the indifference many outside the church feel about us, it cannot be the job of our communities to learn to speak church. It must be the job of the church to learn the dialect of their communities and learn to speak it.

Some churches find themselves in neighborhoods that have transitioned to a whole new demographic. It could be Hispanic families living where once Anglo families lived. Formerly working-class neighborhoods are being overrun by young singles with a taste for gourmet coffee. African American families are moving to the suburbs that were previously monochromatic. Some of these transitions bring opportunities, others challenges. There are well-documented issues with a lot of the gentrification happening now with many urban communities. For good or ill, most communities across the United States are in shift. Even in rural places, once thriving school systems are being downsized as families move out and newer retirees move in.

Even if the folks outside your church doors still look mostly like you, the unavoidable truth is that many of the folks you encounter are not interested in your church and the things you do. Not to say all, but the rapidly expanding group of nones and dones won't be entering your doors no matter how clever your front sign is.

When we talk to people about church we too often fall into the *features and benefits* trap. Features and Benefits (F&B) was a term coined for mid-twentieth century advertising. You convince people to buy your product by telling them about all the great things about it. It was understood you don't need to educate people about soap, only why yours is the best soap. Everybody uses soap, after all.

The church has been operating out of a similar mentality for years. Our outreach efforts, when we do them at all, focus on how good our Sunday school is, how great the preaching is, and how bright our Christmas Eve service candles are. We are still operating out of a time when if you could offer a better experience than the church down the road then you'd expect to grow. We love to talk about the F&B of our worship and ministries. Unfortunately, most of us now live in communities where people have never experienced soap or have decided they no longer care about it.

If we continue to talk about F&B as we have, we will continue to speak in a language less and less people can hear. We know what we mean when we say Bible study or Sunday school, but those outside of us have no clue and words like "study" or "school" are not that enticing. For lots of us, how we talk about what we do is as critical as what we are doing.

The word *school* puts pictures in our minds of neatly organized rows of desks and a chalkboard up front. I've even seen churches use clip art with that exact scene in it to advertise their Sunday school. Yet, I have not seen a Sunday school class in years that is organized that way. Many churches have gone to interactive experiences that involve art, music, and play. School is no longer an appropriate term for these activities, but we persist with it because it is what we are used to. I have also never run into a child, after experiencing Monday through Friday school, who was super excited to add another day.

When Sunday school first started, the term *school* was considered a good thing. It began in communities where child labor was prevalent and most children lacked the opportunity to attend traditional school. Sunday school was created to teach reading and writing through scripture. Parents were eager to sign their children up for reasons of literacy not just religion.[6]

Bible studies suffer from similar naming issues. Adults are still seeking meaning in life, now as ever, but increasingly that meaning comes from shared experiences with others, not just from reading and reflection. The best Bible study groups make shared experience part of what they do, but the word "study" conjures up images of books stacked high on tables with people quietly joined around. If we are honest, in many of the longtime Bible studies we find in our churches, the actual study part is secondary to the coffee and conversation shared before and after. Folks are primarily gathered to see their friends and for much-needed social interactions.

It is past time we look at what we are doing and ask ourselves two very important sets of questions. First, is this activity helping us fulfill our why? Is it bringing people into contact with God's grace and love? Is it making room for that love and grace to be transformational?

Second, are we communicating effectively about our it? Are we talking features and benefits using church language and assumptions? Have we given the nones and dones any reason to care about what we are doing?

These two sets of questions are critical to being the witnesses God calls us to be. If we are not offering

---

[6] For a good overview of the beginnings of the Sunday School movement visit:
https://en.wikipedia.org/wiki/Sunday_school.

authentic encounters with God then we are not true witnesses. If we are not speaking in a language our neighbors can understand, we are not true witnesses either.

A group at Harvard Divinity School released the results of a study about where people are finding community and meaning in the world today. They called it *How We Gather*, and it, along with their follow up work, offers important insights. Nones and dones are not flocking to our churches but they are going other places like CrossFit, SoulCycle, and dinner gatherings. In their work the research team uncovered six pervasive themes in these gathering places that are easily recognizable and translatable into the world of church as we know it. Those themes are:

- Community
- Personal Transformation
- Social Transformation
- Purpose Finding
- Creativity
- Accountability

While each theme isn't equally present in all the places covered by the study, these six themes offer insights about the deeper meaning people are finding in these places. Several are fitness related, but are not gyms as we conventionally know them. Instead, they are places where the opportunity for exercise is mixed with motivational activities and community. These

---

[7] See www.howwegather.org.

organizations have discovered that people aren't interested in working out to simply be healthy, they are looking to transform themselves in some way and recognize that being part of a community is beneficial to that.

Others focus on social change and our basic human need to make the world a better place. Folks are seeking to be part of social transformation and work for justice through networks created to do good.

While the church has shied away from accountability as a focus in recent decades, it is interesting to see how many of the up-and-coming organizations have embraced it. While not covered in this study, the long-standing organization Alcoholics Anonymous places accountability at the center of its work. Not in an overbearing way, but through the twelve steps, regular group meetings, and sponsors, there are overlapping layers that keep people progressing toward sobriety.

Let's briefly look at each of these themes to see how they correspond to church life.

Community

What is a church if not a community of faith? Community is at the heart of what we do and there can be no church without it. Though we often confuse church with the building the community gathers in, we all know that the church that God intends is made of up people, not bricks. In many ways people are like other pack animals: we feel more safe around others we trust. Everyone craves community and the church is not the church without it.

As Christians we believe in a relational God. God is not distant or disinterested in our lives. We believe that the purpose of life is to be in relationship with God and one another. That is why behavior or practices that degrade community are so toxic in the church. Scripture is full of prohibitions against gossiping, lying, and cheating one another. The Ten Commandments are a basic do and don't list for living in community.

The type of community the church is after is not one of shallow interactions but deep relationship. Yet I fear many churches today are more the former than the latter. To form deep relationships there must be trust and a willingness to accept difference. In a church I served, a young, naturally shy man read scripture for us one morning. To do so, he had to conquer his own fears about speaking in public and do something he was not really comfortable doing. He did a fine job, but later I heard complaints because he was wearing a hat while he did it. Someone left him an anonymous letter about his apparent transgression and suddenly trust was broken. He no longer felt connected to the community and left the church shortly after.

There are some who are so connected to our churches that no force of nature could break them of it. Yet for many, including any nones and dones you are lucky enough to encounter, their connection is fresh and delicate. We need to tend and care for these relationships and not let them fall victim to petty differences. This is likely one of the most difficult things for an existing church to learn: how to be truly hospitable and nurture tentative attachments into strong bonds. If we can learn to do that well, we can learn to nurture the type of community God intends for our churches to be.

Personal Transformation

The self-help section continues to be a large part of most bookstores. Every day there is a new book that promises the trimmer body, better behaved children, and the more loving marriage we all want. Facebook and reality TV have left us all craving more out of our lives, while younger people opt for memorable experiences rather than fine china. Personal transformation isn't about narcissism or selfishness; it's a healthy need that is about recognizing we are all works in progress.

Personal transformation takes many forms and focuses on developing our bodies, minds, and spirits. The church has laid claim to spiritual improvement but we can no longer ignore that all three of these areas are deeply connected. It is cruel to offer a hungry person a Bible but no food. In addition, mental illness is real and the church has a role to play breaking down the stigma around it.

Churches have often hosted AA and other support groups but rarely embrace that type of work as core to their identity. There is so much opportunity today, as one in ten people have diabetes, and with other chronic illnesses on the rise, for churches to be places of support for those struggling with these issues. With addiction, illness, loneliness, PTSD, and moral injury all around us, the church must learn to look beyond spiritual health to holistic health because it is all deeply interwoven.

Development of one's spiritual life may be the most natural place for the church to be, but even there we need to cautious not to play it too safe. We can no longer afford feel-good sermons and shallow theology. Spiritual improvement requires fresh and profound experiences with God that challenge our assumptions and expose our prejudices. We know better than ever there are no easy answers to life's challenges and church of all places needs to name that reality.

Social Transformation

As social beings who crave community we care about the space we inhabit. Sympathy and empathy are so fundamental to human nature that those that lack them are diagnosed with medical conditions. It is no wonder we are motivated to action by stories of hungry children or oppressed workers. Our species simply could not survive if we were not invested in improving the situation of others. For followers of Jesus, social transformation is the living embodiment of the call to love our neighbors.

While each individual is capable of profound good, our ability to effect change increases dramatically as more people join the cause. Social transformation is about creating networks for good that involve many in the blessing of others. In the earliest incarnation of the church one of the first tasks undertaken was to form a network of support for orphans and widows. The book of Acts and the letters of Paul talk about the collection that was taken up for their support. As with personal transformation, social transformation is an inseparable part of who we are.

We often talk in the church about acts of mercy and justice. These are two separate but related notions. Acts of mercy are about addressing the needs we see in front of us, like feeding a hungry person or comforting someone in crisis. Justice, on the other hand, is about confronting the systems that disadvantage one group over another and holding people accountable for the harm they have done to others. Mercy and justice are woven into the earliest fabric of our faith as Micah 6:8 famously states it:

He has told you, O mortal, what is good; and what does the Lord require of you but to do justice, and to love kindness, and to walk humbly with your God?

Churches do not collect food for the hungry, visit the sick in the hospital, advocate for the rights of the poor, and call out injustice because we are nice people. It is not a side project of the church we engage in simply because we like it and it feels good. It is essential to who we are. It is surprising to me how many people I encounter in the church, even those who work for the church, who have no clue our primary mission is to make the world a better place.

But it is! Call it social transformation, call it bringing about God's kingdom, call it what you like, the truth is the church is not the church if we aren't engaged in this work.

Purpose Finding

One of the things I had to get used to when I entered ministry was people asking me to share my call story. It is an expectation of clergy that we should be able to recount a tale of how God entered our lives and personally summoned us to a life set apart. The first time I encountered this, on my second day of seminary, I had no clue what they were asking for. I felt left out as my peers tearfully recounted how the Holy Spirit had moved them to accept a call to be a pastor. I was left wondering, did I have a call? Had I missed something? If there was a burning bush in my past, I had certainly missed it.

"Call" in the church is an interesting thing. We often relate it to clergy but it's hard not to notice that most stories in scripture seem far more interested in normal folks. When religious leaders show up at all it's usually because they are messing things up. None of the twelve disciples were religious leaders. Most of the Old Testament prophets or heroes weren't either. We do a disservice to everyone when we assume a call to be a pastor is somehow better than a call to be a nurse, teacher, lawyer, accountant, mechanic, or plumber. God's kingdom needs all the people and a church that fails to recognize that does the kingdom a large disservice.

Any healthy church will help people relate their vocations, hobbies, and interests to God's work in the world. Instead we seem to persist with a false dichotomy of sacred and secular. We designate things as Christian music, Christian books, and Christian movies. Like God can't show up in the weekend top 40 countdown? Ridiculous! Our bold claim is that our God is the God of the whole universe. This fake sacred/secular divide causes us to think that God is somehow more interested in what happens at church than what happens at our workplaces or homes. Again, ridiculous! God knows even better than us that it is out in the world amongst the people where the Holy Spirit most often shows up.

The up-and-coming generation is getting a reputation for being job hoppers. Many don't stay more than three to five years in a job. Interestingly, when they are surveyed they say they aren't leaving for more money or better benefits. Instead, they are leaving because they don't feel like they are making a difference, or don't believe in the mission of the company. Think about that. Purpose is so important for these folks that they make major life changes over it. Similarly, when these same people believe in the mission of a place and have a deep sense they are an important part of living out that mission, they become deeply loyal. The church is uniquely situated, with our focus on love of God and neighbor, to help people discern what gifts and talents they have and where they can share them.

Creativity

All humans have a need to feel understood. Part of this is our need to create things and express ourselves. We love to create beauty and share it with others. Creativity may be expressed in expected ways like painting, singing, or drawing. It may also be expressed in unexpected ways. When I was a software developer there was often nothing more beautiful to me than a well-crafted algorithm. Solving a problem in an elegant way was a cause for celebration. Today my creative passion is funneled into my love of cooking. We often have people over to dinner specifically so I have the excuse to spend an entire afternoon in the kitchen exploring and creating.

There are so many opportunities in any church to support creative outlets for people. Worship is the obvious one, but so is Sunday school[8], missions, and really any program we do. At my previous church I did a summer worship series on Moses. Each week had a different theme and I wanted a visual representation of the theme each week that would build over time. We had a creative individual in the church and I asked her to help. I gave her the planned scriptures and gave her permission to use whatever she felt called to, to express the theme. It was amazing! One Sunday as I entered what I thought was the empty sanctuary I about leapt out of my skin as a mannequin in full Egyptian garb greeted me on the

[8] Just don't call it "Sunday School."

front stage.

The challenge in releasing the creativity of people is to give enough direction so they know what they are supposed to do, but not so much that it becomes paint by numbers. So much life now is fill in the blanks. Few people truly get to engage their imaginations at work or at home. Giving them the chance to do that is a true gift.

Accountability

John Wesley, founder of the Methodist movement, was a strong believer in accountability. He organized his followers into small groups called classes and bands. The primary purpose of these groups was to watch over each other as people grew in their faith together. While the *How We Gather* study uses the word accountability, I prefer the word encouragement because that is what we are after. It is not about tearing people down but building people up. Intentional encouragement like you find from personal trainers or physical therapists is key to the church. Yes, you may need to offer a correction or two along the way, but your goal is not to hold people to a proscribed standard. Instead we encourage people to more fully be who God created them to be.

Accountability/encouragement is critical to the future of the church. Unfortunately, lots of us get it wrong. For many, accountability means the creation of a set of well-documented standards that we can use to easily determine if people are living by them. It also includes some understanding of what the consequences are for not following the standards. It is a system of rules and punishments meant to keep everyone in line. You don't need to look any further than the first books of the Bible, and most notably the ten commandments, to understand what this looks like. The advantage of this is that it is simple and not much thought is required. All you have to do is go down the list of do's and don'ts and make sure you have all the boxes checked.

Unfortunately, this not the way Jesus wants us to live. Jesus calls us to a higher place where we worry less about black-and-white rules but instead focus on the larger work of loving God and neighbor. Take the following story from Mark as an example.

Mark 10:17-22

As he was setting out on a journey, a man ran up and knelt before him, and asked him, "Good Teacher, what must I do to inherit eternal life?" Jesus said to him, "Why do you call me good? No one is good but God alone. You know the commandments: 'You shall not murder; You shall not commit adultery; You shall not steal; You shall not bear false witness; You shall not defraud; Honor your father and mother.'" He said to him, "Teacher, I have kept all these since my youth." Jesus, looking at him, loved him and said, "You lack one thing; go, sell what you own, and give the money to the poor, and you will have treasure in heaven; then come, follow me." When he heard this, he was shocked and went away grieving, for he had many possessions.

I've noticed the line, "go, sell what you own, and

give the money to the poor," rarely comes up in conversations about the inerrancy of scripture or following all the standards in the bible. Not sure why that is?

Seriously though. The person who came up to Jesus truly believed he was on the right path. He had checked all the do and don't boxes and assumed he was all set. And by the standards of the Hebrew Bible texts Jesus quotes, he was. Yet Jesus also understood that the standards he quotes were never meant to be an exhaustive list. Instead those early black-and-white standards were the foundation stones of the larger, more nuanced, and just kingdom God is building.

Notice scripture goes to pains to make sure that while Jesus is rebuking him we know he is doing it in love. Jesus knows that, for the man, his relationship with money and his wealth is more important to him than our shared call to love God and love our neighbors. So, Jesus encourages him. He sees the man is adhering to the letter of the law while missing the spirit of it entirely.

Accountability must always come in an environment of mutual respect and love. We are not judges or juries sent to pass judgement on others. Instead, our role is most similar to that of a personal trainer. Our job is to help people progress on their individual walk of faith and recognize it may not look the same as ours. We are to be first and foremost encouragers. People need to know that their progress is important and it matters to others as well as themselves. We all need tangible reminders that God loves us too much to simply leave us as we are. We are all works in progress.

This isn't to say we don't sometimes need to call a spade a spade. Those involved in behaviors that are harmful to themselves or others may need a reminder to first do no harm. But this again must be done in the context of unequivocal love for the person.

These six themes give us a new way to think about the many things we are already doing in our churches. Think about something that gives you life in your church, some place or time where you have felt the movement the Holy Spirit. Can you relate that experience to one or more of the themes above?

Let's talk a little about community. For most of the last half of the twentieth century the church's primary theme was community. As people moved into suburbs church was a way to get us out of our tract homes and garages. As we started to drive everywhere instead of walk it was the place we got to actually see our neighbors on a regular basis. Other social organizations flourished during this time, too, like the Elks, Eagles, and Masons. Connecting us together into community was something people needed.

At this same time, it became popular for teenagers to designated a road in town as the "drag." A Friday or Saturday evening would often start with putting a few friends in a car and taking a few laps of the local drag. No matter what town you were in the drag always featured one thing in common: it looped back on itself. You would go one direction on a street then turn around and go the opposite direction on the same street. Why? So you could see who else was out. The drag was an organizational technique for creating ad hoc community for the evening. The church played the same role.

The drag in the small town I grew up in is gone and so are most of the rest. The road is still there but you won't find teenagers taking laps anymore. All the community they need is attainable through texting and Snapchat. The drag is obsolete technology. A church that focuses solely on basic community may find itself in the same place. That is why it's imperative to look at more themes than just the first.

Let's think about worship again if for no other reason than it is something that all churches do. What themes are present in your worship? Notice, none of the themes is about entertainment. We are not Netflix and we couldn't possibly compete with Netflix if we wanted to. Worship is about something other than entertaining people. What would it look like if personal transformation was a focus of your worship time? I recently visited a new church start in Parker, Colorado who had their highest Sunday attendance of the month during a blizzard! Why? Because during the worship time they were packing lunches for a local youth organization. During the service! They were involved in social transformation while they worshiped and people came out while the rest of the area was closed because of snow! This is how powerful aligning your activities with the themes above can be and how well it translates to a wider audience.

What is important to start thinking about is why you do what you do and how you could communicate that to others without defaulting to church speak. If we are to be effective witnesses, we must take on the challenge of translating our whys into words the masses around us can understand. If the Holy Spirit showed up 2000 years ago to help this happen, we have every right to think the Holy Spirit will show up to help us. We just need to ask.

Get to Work

In this section we identified some critical ideas. Everyone has felt needs. We all have things inside of us that pull us in various directions. Some of them are good, like the drive to help out when we see someone struggling. Some of them are less good or even unhealthy, like drinking too much or going into large amounts of debt to acquire things. The church exists to help support people in meeting the good needs and resisting the bad ones. This is a bit simplistic, obviously, but helpful.

The categories we discussed in this chapter are really all about our needs as humans. Reconsider the list of categories and ask the current activities of your church. List your activities under the needs it is trying to meet.

Community

Personal Transformation

Social Transformation

Purpose Finding

Creativity

Accountability

Many churches will be well represented in the Community area and less well represented elsewhere. This is a problem because in the age of Facebook and text messages community is easy to come by. If a church wants to really meet the nones and dones, it will need something beyond community to get people's attention. Not that community isn't important; it is! People won't stick around if they don't become part of the community. But it also won't be a starting place for most people. You need to speak to other categories as well.

4. That One Church

Whenever I spend time with a church in my role as the vital church guy, invariably I have some version of the same conversation. Someone will ask if I've heard of XYZ church in the area. This is the church that is bucking the trend of church decline and seems to be full of people. Usually, coveted young people. They always want to know why that church is so full and theirs is not.

Much ink and bits have been spilled around this topic. Typically, we hear reasons like:

- Because they have a band.
- Because they have a playground.
- Because they preach the "correct" gospel.
- Because the pastor went to this or that seminary (or didn't go at all).
- Because they feel this or that way about a hot social issue.

Many people attempt to lay claim to these growing churches as a way to rally support for their particular cause. They want to use these growing churches as a way to advance their agenda. I have heard all the above and more bandied about as the reason XYZ church is growing and, reciprocally, why our church is not. Of course all of it misses the point entirely. None of these things is the reason.

There are plenty of churches with traditional style worship that are growing. There are progressive churches in the Bible Belt growing. There are conservative churches on the west coast that are growing. Whatever criteria we think is the magic fix to make our churches attractive to the nones and the dones will let us down. There is no magic fix.

The truth about those churches, and the differences between them and most churches in decline, is that those churches value and invest in relationships. They grow because it is a priority for them – often the highest priority. These are churches that are willing to adapt themselves to accommodate the needs and desires of those outside the church. They are willing to focus on those needs and desires above the preferences of those in the church already. That is the exact opposite of what you find in most declining churches where the preferences of those currently attending reign supreme.

You should be saying to yourself about now, "Wait a minute, didn't you tell us church growth wasn't the point of evangelism?" Why yes, yes I did. And I stand by that. What most miss in looking at all the XYZ churches is that there is healthy growth and unhealthy growth. Many of those churches we look at with envy are built more to satisfy the ego of the pastor than to serve the good news. Others have become so performance oriented that worship is more like a concert than a communal experience of the Holy Spirit. Just because a church is growing numerically doesn't mean they are doing things right or for the right reasons. While it is true growth can be a sign of health, like when plants and animals grow, we can't forget that cancer grows, too, and that is not a good thing.

As someone who has struggled with weight most of my life I am very confused by the idea of losing weight. Should I expect to wake up some morning having misplaced twenty pounds? Because in my experience that never happens. Instead, I know there are lots of factors that go into decreasing my weight, including diet, exercise, medications I take, and my genetics. If decreasing weight is my goal, I will be disappointed because it simply isn't possible all on its own. Decreasing weight done right is a byproduct of investing in a healthier lifestyle. Done wrong, it leads to eating disorders or similar conditions.

Growth in the church is the same. It is a byproduct of investing in a healthy church lifestyle. It can also be achieved in unhealthy ways, but only to the long-term detriment of the church. As said before, evangelism isn't primarily about church growth. That said, when evangelism is done right, growth becomes a likely byproduct.

1 Thessalonians 2:5-12

As you know and as God is our witness, we never came with words of flattery or with a pretext for greed; nor did we seek praise from mortals, whether from you or from others, though we might have made demands as apostles of Christ. But we were gentle among you, like a nurse tenderly caring for her own children. So deeply do we care for you that we are determined to share with you not only the gospel of God but also our own selves, because you have become very dear to us.

You remember our labor and toil, brothers and sisters; we worked night and day, so that we might not burden any of you while we proclaimed to you the gospel of God. You are witnesses, and God also, how pure, upright, and blameless our conduct was toward you believers. As you know, we dealt with each one of you like a father with his children, urging and encouraging you and pleading that you should lead a life worthy of God, who calls you into his own kingdom and glory.

In this passage the apostle Paul is writing to a church in a town called Thessalonica. He is reminding them of the time he and his team were with them helping them build a new church. Almost no one had heard of this person named Jesus at this time. Like today's nones and dones they had no real knowledge of Jesus or, as mostly gentiles, any real knowledge of Judaism. Paul's opportunity was then very similar to ours: introducing people for the first time to God and God's son Jesus. Paul is never shy to speak of his accomplishments for God and here we see that on full display. He has no issue reminding them of how he and his team acted, and it is obvious he has a high opinion of what they did. This is important for us because people are still people and prefer to be treated well.

Paul reminds them that they came only with the motive of sharing the good news. He points out that they had no pretext of greed, meaning they weren't there for their own gain or to solicit donations. Paul will, in fact, make a request later for the support of the Christian movement. The book of Acts talks about this collection and how it was brought back to Jerusalem for the good of the movement. Yet this was not his motivation and we are left to imagine that even if this collection were never taken, Paul would still be invested in these people and their journey of faith. It must be the same with us today. A healthy church is one that is invested in the faith development of their people and the development of all those they encounter. If we are driven by finances, people will see through it in an instant.

Paul is also quick to point out that this work takes a great deal of energy and time. He is not afraid of hard work and he recognizes that he, as the messenger, must do the heavy lifting. He celebrates the hard work that he did as a way to set an expectation for those he is writing to. The first step in living a healthy church lifestyle is to recognize that doing so will take time and energy. There are no easy fixes, only the time-tested work of building new relationships with new people. Doing so for the love of those people and no other reason.

Throughout Paul's letters we read about the trials he went through to bring the message of Jesus to the world around him. Some of his letters were written from prison and he talks more than once about beatings he endured.

Paul was a leader of one of those growing XYZ churches. He was very successful in reaching people with the good news, so much so that jealousy brewed between him and other members of the early Christian movement. It is also what landed him in hot water with local authorities who put him in jail. At this time there was nobody more important than Caesar, and those loyal to Caesar took issue with anyone organizing people around a higher authority.

None of us are likely to be put in prison or beaten for our faith, but we can't pretend our faith won't cost us something. The time and energy you invest in evangelism will need to come from somewhere. You will likely need to stop doing some things you currently do to make room for the new tasks ahead of you. It's important to take some time and think about what you are really willing to invest. I don't say this to scare you, only to be realistic. I also need to assure you beyond any doubt you will experience blessing for being Christ's witnesses. That doesn't mean you'll get rich like some TV preachers may promise, but you will see God show up and do amazing things. And that is a priceless gift.

Celebrate, Please!

One the greatest challenges to reaching new people is our unwillingness to celebrate in a public way where God is acting in our church. I subscribe to many church email newsletters and recently I came across one that epitomizes this problem. At the top of the email was the calendar of upcoming committee meetings. Below that was a couple paragraphs from the pastor reflecting on something that had nothing to do with their upcoming sermon or relating to anything happening in the world today. Finally, buried at the bottom, in the prayer section, was a prayer request that read, "Prayers of thanksgiving for the 300 housing insecure people fed at our annual free community meal."

Three hundred people fed and it's buried at the bottom of the email! What?!

Many of our churches are involved in life-changing ministry now but someone could attend every Sunday service for a month and never know it. People could read newsletters for a year and often have no idea how God's grace is made real to people though the church's ministry. Why is this? Why are we so willing to hide our good deeds that the larger public is left to wonder what value churches add to their community? Jesus himself has some advice for us on this one.

Matthew 5:14-16

You are the light of the world. A city built on a hill cannot be hidden. No one after lighting a lamp puts it under the bushel basket, but on the lampstand, and it gives light to all in the house. In the same way, let your light shine before others, so that they may see your good works and give glory to your Father in heaven.

I've visited churches where the first few minutes of every worship service was spent reminding folks of all the amazing ministry happening in the church. It was a cheerleading session intended to remind people of what they were a part of. Where most churches do announcements, this church was celebrating where God showed up in the week through the people of faith who called that church home.

If we want to reach those around us, we first must reach those already in our pews. People need to believe, truly believe, that they are part of something bigger than themselves that is full of life. A mentor early in my ministry told me to find at least one thing my church was doing to bless the community and then "preach the heck out of it." No matter how small, never let people forget they are part of something special and important. No pastor should give a sermon that doesn't include at least one reference to how their local church is involved in blessing others. We must stoke the spark until the light shines bright. Then we must shine that light in our communities.

Your first task is to evangelize those already in your church so that when they encounter new people they are on fire for the place they worship. Now, we need to be real here. Not everyone is going to get on board with this. They'll say things like *we shouldn't be flashy* or *that's not appropriate*. Someone will inevitably quote the next chapter of Matthew where Jesus says, "Beware of practicing your piety before others in order to be seen by them; for then you have no reward from your Father in heaven." (Matthew 6:1). When they do they'll be right, but not how they think.

To understand we need to look at the audience of Matthew five and six. In chapter five, which is the beginning of the sermon on the mount, Jesus is addressing the gathered crowd. In Greek, he uses the plural you when he says "You are the light of the world." If y'all was appropriate for biblical translation this would be the perfect place to us it. In chapter six when Jesus says, "Beware of practicing your piety…" he switches to the singular you. Here he is talking to individuals in the larger group.

Jesus wants us to show the world what God is up to so long as it is about demonstrating God's goodness and not our ego. In Matthew six Jesus is speaking against the all-too-common practice of self-righteousness. We are not to wave our individual good deeds in front of others so that they will think we are somehow better than them. This, I hope we all agree, is something we should avoid. At the same time, we as a group cannot be afraid to shine the light God has given us. As strongly as Jesus argues against self-righteousness he argues for us being witnesses to God's action in our lives and the life of our churches.

A church I served as pastor, after a small group spent a great deal of time in prayer, decided to collaborate with some other churches in our area to start a free store. This is a place with clothing and household items that anyone can come to and take what they need. We took over part of the education wing that was unused and collected the remainders of church garage sales to fill it. We got racks donated by a closed thrift shop and, all told, spent a great amount of time and almost no money getting it started. When it came time to have our grand opening one of the greatest struggles we had was convincing the team it was okay to call the local paper and ask them to do a story about us. The challenge was, while several folks worked hard to bring to store to life, all were hesitant to be the public face of it. Not because they were in any way embarrassed by what we were doing; far from it. Instead, the humility the world presses into us had taken over. Thankfully we overcame and the newspaper did come. It provided a great jump start to the ministry as we served over fifty families that first day.

As the years went on and the ministry grew I talked about it every time I could. We were in the local newspaper a couple more times, I was invited to talk at the local Optimist club, and at the school next to our church. At regional and national United Methodist events I shared the story of our free store and the amazing all-volunteer group that ran it. In the first year alone we gave away an estimated $70,000 worth of goods and I made sure everyone in our church knew it. It was the first page of the report to our annual church business meeting.

This is also the time I encountered something else

as I shared the way God was working through our church to bless people. It started out subtly then grew more explicit. Leaders of other churches were getting annoyed with me and my constant sharing about the free store, or the free meal and prison ministry that followed it. At an international conference years later I would learn from an Australian team that this phenomenon has a name: tall poppy syndrome. With tall poppies, ones that stand higher than the rest, the temptation is to cut them down to size. Standing out too much is considered antisocial to some and not something to be celebrated. If my motivation had been to share my greatness as a pastor, the crowd would have a point. But, very sincerely, it wasn't. My hope was for our church to shine light in our community and for us to be true witnesses to God's grace. That meant, as the pastor, at times, I was called on to be the chief spokesperson for us. Truly it's far better when the volunteers and clients can tell their own story, but even then my job is to create a space for them to do that. It's an unavoidable responsibility of being a pastor in the church.

My prayer has always been that when other church leaders encountered stories like ours they would not mumble about us disparagingly, but instead take it as permission to notice and celebrate where God is working in their churches. Then, begin to speak about it! It is little wonder so many people today are indifferent about the church. Even when we are doing the right things we hide them away from the public. We all must urgently get over this collective false modesty and not be afraid to tell our story. Because in the end it's not even our story, it's God's story!

For Pastors and Key Leaders

If you are a pastor or a key lay leader in your church this work has to start with you. You have the power to give permission to others to start seeing and celebrating what God is up to. Here, though, people will only follow by example. People need to see and experience celebration firsthand. You must model it for them. In the next couple chapters we will talk about techniques for getting the word out, but for that to be effective you first have to have a word to share. So be on the lookout for God at work.

Before you look at doing new things, look at what you are already doing. It is far easier to adapt processes already underway than start new things from scratch.

The Sermon

The death of the sermon has been long been reported but never realized. To me, the popularity of TED talks[9] shows that the format of a fifteen- to twenty-five minute topical speech is far from over. In fact, it lends itself well to the popular mediums of YouTube and podcasts. I have been out of the weekly worship business for a while but I still run into people who tell me they listened to the podcast of my

---

[9] www.TED.com

sermons. What is dying quickly is tolerance for poorly crafted sermons. There is simply too much quality content at our fingertips and it has made us all sophisticated listeners. My practice was to listen to at least two other quality preachers a week when I was leading a local church. All regular preachers should do this.

The sermon is your chance each week to help people learn to see God at work. Each sermon should contain at least one real, relatable story of the Holy Spirit's moving. The free store was open two Saturdays a month. The Sunday morning after I would always find some of the volunteers before worship and ask if anything cool had happened the day before. Nine times out of ten I would hear something amazing and I would find a way to work it into the sermon. Sometimes I would have to say, "This has nothing to do with today's sermon, but I heard a story you have to hear." Another frequent occurrence was for the person who told me the story to come up after service and say how much they appreciated being included. Oftentimes they themselves were not even seeing God at work; they just saw it as something neat that had happened. As the spiritual leader of that community, it was my job to frame things in terms of God's grace and love. The more I did that, the more they learned to do it themselves.

The Newsletter

If you do a regular newsletter, either paper or electronic, you would likely be surprised how much it gets read by those who receive it, especially by older members. For internal evangelism this is a great tool. It isn't valuable, though, if it's full of meeting notices and birthday lists. Not that those can't be in there, but they shouldn't be front page. Every newsletter should contain a story (with pictures) of how your church is blessing the community. Preferably written by a layperson involved in the ministry. It should also include an invitation for a way to get involved. If you are part of a larger denomination, include a national or international article on something your denomination is involved with. My denomination provides regular news articles and I have never been turned down when I've asked permission to republish the article in our newsletter. Finally, anyone reading your newsletter should come away inspired and feeling like they are part of something important.

Over 100 times the bible tells us to *fear not* in one form or another. It's like God knows that our default reaction to the unexpected is to cower. Yet if we are to be the light-bearing witnesses God asks us to be, we cannot help but court the unexpected. We simply can't know how people will react to us or which efforts will bear fruit. So we have no choice but to move beyond fear and trust the Holy Spirit.

We have to invest time and resources in cultivating new relationships. We can't make people care the way we need them to, but we can inspire them to learn to care. Finally, we must recognize that for these efforts to succeed they must be led by those who have one hundred percent bought into the idea that God is moving in the world and begging our churches to be part of it. Once we start to develop these things the rest is simple.

Get to Work

You will need to make room for the new practices of evangelism your team needs to take on. So, what will you stop doing to make room for the things you should be doing?

How are you going to celebrate the work God is doing in your church? It cannot be overstated how important this is. For people to really experience God's love in the way we hope they will, they must first recognize when God is working in their midst. Modeling this by celebrating the way God is moving in your church is the best way to teach this skill. God is in the big things and the small things, so be on the lookout for both.

Worship is a good time to celebrate in any church. As you plan each service ask yourself these questions:

1. How will people know God is alive and moving in today's worship?

2. How will people know they are part of building God's beloved community by being part of this church?
3. How will people learn to see God at work in their lives through what we are doing today?

You can ask the same questions about your newsletter, Facebook page, or marketing material. These questions should be part of any quality check for anything you do along with checking spelling and grammar.

You simply cannot do this enough. Do it every week! Every week remind people of how God is moving and show them what celebrating God's love and grace looks like.

5. Make it a Job

Acts 6:1-7

Now during those days, when the disciples were increasing in number, the Hellenists complained against the Hebrews because their widows were being neglected in the daily distribution of food. And the twelve called together the whole community of the disciples and said, "It is not right that we should neglect the word of God in order to wait at tables. Therefore, friends, select from among yourselves seven men of good standing, full of the Spirit and of wisdom, whom we may appoint to this task, while we, for our part, will devote ourselves to prayer and to serving the word." What they said pleased the whole community, and they chose Stephen, a man full of faith and the Holy Spirit, together with Philip, Prochorus, Nicanor, Timon, Parmenas, and Nicolaus, a proselyte of Antioch. They had these men stand before the apostles, who prayed and laid their hands on them.

The word of God continued to spread; the number of the disciples increased greatly in Jerusalem, and a great many of the priests became obedient to the faith.

It is a temptation to say *it's everyone's job to make new relationships*. Meaning, evangelism is everyone's job. We are all called to be witnesses, after all. Yes, this is true. But if you come from a church that currently does not have a robust system of evangelism, statements like this are problematic. Simply put, if it's everyone's job then it's nobody's job. Somebody has to go first; you will not get everyone to go at once. Think of it this way. When a train is first getting started there is some slack left between the cars. This means the engine isn't trying to get all the cars moving at once. That would be impossible. Instead it gets one going a few inches, then two, then three, and so on. You are the first few cars in the train; you have to get moving first.

In the early church, as the Christian movement grew, it became apparent that responsibility would need to be shared between more people. At first the disciples were trying to be evangelists, chaplains, and community organizers all at the same time. The passage above recounts when they first started to empower new leaders in the community and share leadership responsibilities. And what was the response? The community grew! It's important to realize your pastor can't be your chaplain, CEO, and sole evangelist for your church. It simply won't work. You need a dedicated group of people full of faith and the Holy Spirit like in Acts chapter six. If you are reading this book, that likely is you.

Churches can have all the strategy and mission statements they want, but if they don't have a culture of getting out in the world and trying things, it won't matter. Business management guru Peter Drucker said, "Culture eats strategy for breakfast," and that is just as true in the church as it is in the business world. In the Acts passage above the disciples are not just delegating tasks; they are defining a culture that has two important characteristics. First, they are sharing leadership and responsibility. The disciples would have every right to presume that they, as the ones who were actually with Jesus, should have final say. But they don't do that. Instead they share authority and responsibility with others as new leaders are raised up in the movement. The other important thing they do is make the highest priority the outward mission to "serve the world." They know beyond any doubt if they want God's grace and love to be known, it has to be the highest priority of the movement they are beginning.

This is not to say that caring for those inside the movement isn't important. Far from it. Notice they pick seven people "full of the Spirit and of wisdom" to continue that work. In Christian communities we must recognize the need to treat each other with dignity and respect and do all we can to meet the needs of our brothers and sisters. At the same time, we are not simply a club for mutual support. Our purpose is greater than that.

If your church is going to be successful in shifting to an outward-focused culture the only way to get that done is for a small group of people to start living that way and then spread the change. At first this group will likely encounter resistance and you will learn quickly how many people are stuck in the current ways of doing things. This is to be expected and, in fact, can be a sign you are on the right path. As time progresses, and as the Holy Spirit is increasingly noticed, energy and momentum will build. Soon, as more train cars are moving, the force becomes irresistible.

At this point my prayer is that you and your team are convinced you have an important mission to fulfill. Your community is the mission field that God has given you and it is waiting for witnesses of God's love and grace. It's time to be serious about reaching them. So the question I hope you are asking is, how?

To do this work you will need a team that acts like a team, not a committee. Teams are about taking action and accomplishing things first and foremost. This is what makes them different from committees. If team members are not leaving your meetings with tasks to accomplish then you are not acting as a team. This cannot be about just *talking* about things; it must be about *doing* things.

Start in Prayer

Everything should be done in prayer. You must be able to say with confidence that you believe you are following the leading of the Holy Spirit in whatever you do. Many of us are not practiced in doing this and it will take time to learn how to do it well. At first it will seem awkward; that's okay. Stick with it. There are some techniques you can try to get you started. Over time you will learn to adapt to your team's unique needs and gifts.

Each meeting should have a significant spiritual development component at the beginning lasting at least twenty minutes. Don't shortchange this. Praying the local news is a great way to start. This is a small group experience that you can do at the start of your meeting. For this activity you start in prayer specifically asking God to open your minds and hearts to God's working in your community. Then you take a newspaper or online local news site and ask each person to skim until something catches their eye. Each person should read the article and while they do ask themselves two questions:

1. Where is God working in this?
2. How can our church bring grace and love to this situation?

The answer to question two should not be starting a brand-new ministry. That is a recipe for moving a dozen directions at once and getting nowhere. Instead, think in terms of what you may already be doing. How can it be adapted or directed to address what you are reading? How can you use the situation you read about to help people better understand the church and its role in the community?

While writing this I took a moment to pray over my hometown's news site.[10] I noticed an article about the local college doing a week-long event to raise awareness of violence against women. Obviously, this is an issue that should concern anyone in the church who cares about the God-given dignity of all people. As part of a connectional denomination, my church is part of work around the globe addressing these issues. What would it look like for a church in the area to focus worship on these issues, highlight the work we are already a part of, and use their social media presence to raise awareness of these issues and the church's response to them? Piggybacking on the momentum of the event, the church could show another side of itself to the local community that may not be expected.

Praying the news can result in ideas like those above or simply a greater awareness of what is happening in your area and what people are concerned with. Either way it is time well spent and can provide fertile ground for the Holy Spirit to work.

There is no end of other options for your team to pray together. Lectio Divina is popular and can be done in many different ways. However you practice prayer, make it a strong part of all your team meetings.

---

[10] As a member of Generation X I've not read a newspaper in years.

One-on-One

The first relationships to be built will be between your team and members of the community. The team's job is to go first and start moving the train forward. Others will only follow as far as the leaders are willing to go. To help you set a new standard for community relationship building you can start with the tried and true practice of the community one-on-one.

I work with a lot of new church planters, helping to support them in their work. Each of them learns about one-on-ones and are asked to report quarterly how many they have done. Especially early in the life of a project the one-on-ones have turned out to be highly correlated to success in reaching new people. The technique itself is pretty basic.

By now you should have some idea of the why of your church. When doing a one-on-one the goal is to discover the why of the other person. Trey Hall, church planter of Urban Village Church in Chicago, describes it this way: "A relational meeting [one-on-one] is a brief, in-depth exploration into why someone is the way they are: what they give a damn about and why, what keeps them up at night and why, what they hope against hope for in life and why. It's also an opportunity to share those same things about yourself and to look for overlaps. And maybe, depending on the connection, perhaps eventually at another one-on-one in the future, to explore whether you might work together on a common project."[11]

One-on-ones should be no longer than an hour and can happen anywhere. I have purchased a lot of coffee for people doing one-on-ones over my career in ministry. Early in my time at my last church I took the local school principal out for coffee. In those forty minutes I got a better understanding of the challenges at the school and his hopes for his work there. It was exceedingly valuable. My church started to address some key needs and we developed a relationship with several more people at the school. As we became stronger partners the relationship flowed both ways. They allowed us to send advertisements for events like our trunk-or-treat and other not specifically religious happenings. We were also commonly name-dropped in their newsletters and PTA meetings as a helpful partner, a valuable type of word-of-mouth advertising.

Not every one-on-one will lead to fruitful results, but many will. In the end, it's a numbers game. The more you do, the more benefit you will see. Pastors new in communities and churches looking to start a fresh relationship with their neighborhood are encouraged to do as many one-on-ones as possible. One important thing is to always end a one-on-one asking the person for recommendations for who else you should talk to. If a referral sounds good, ask the person to connect you over email or Facebook. This

---

[11] https://recoveringcontrolfreak.org/2016/10/26/a-non-negotiable-practice-for-ministry-leaders/

keeps the cycle going.

I'm a big fan of the show American Pickers on the History Channel. In the show two guys wander the country looking for interesting things to buy from people that they then resell at their stores or at auctions. Many times they "freestyle," meaning they drive around looking for people who look like they might have collected a lot of stuff. Typically the first person they encounter doesn't have what they are looking for. However, they always share with that person who they are and what they care about. They then ask if the person they met knows of anyone else they should talk to. Most often it's this referral that pays off big. It's the same with the one-on-one. The first tier of people you reach out to may not yield much, but the referrals will be invaluable. After all, that first-tier person now knows your why and their brains are by default matching it up with other people they know. Always ask who else you should talk to.

Divide Them Up

Many of us strive to treat people equally. After all, we are all loved equally by God, right? Of course. That said, there are times when we need to recognize different people have different needs so we can't always treat folks one hundred percent the same. One place this is really true is how we communicate. We touched on this a little in chapter three, but now we need to go deeper.

First thing you will need is a system to keep track of people you are trying to reach. This is where a modern church management system comes into play. Previously, these systems were designed to keep the internals of your church running. They tracked numbers and giving and sometimes committee members and meeting rooms. Today, church management systems have become indispensable tools for evangelism, as they help you communicate much more effectively.

You can't build relationships without communicating. So the first thing you need is a place to keep the names and contact information for those your church encounters. Any and all information on any and all people you meet should go in. You also need to decide how you are going to communicate with them. To do that well you need to determine where they are in terms of the strength of their relationship with your church. People who are there every Sunday and serve on all the committees need a different type of communication than someone you met through a community event. Yet many churches communicate the same way to everyone, to their detriment.

It is important to first categorize people. For some this feels wrong. We don't want to be so clinical about it. We need to get over that. People have different needs at different stages of their lives. We are simply recognizing this and showing people greater respect by attempting to be more relevant to where they are.

Most churches would do well adopting four levels of engagement: Prospect, Interested, Involved, Leader. There is a progression through the levels and each requires a slightly different communication approach.

Prospect

These are people that you might have encountered in a community outreach event or were a visitor on Sunday morning. They could also be part of a mailing list you purchased or contact information provided by a friend or family member. What's important is that you know their name and at least one way to contact them (e.g., snail mail, email, or phone). These people don't care about when your next church council meeting is and you shouldn't waste time telling them. These folks need to know your why. If they are going to get interested in your community, they need to know why you do what you do. Why should they care about your church? Why should they want to be involved?

Communication with this group should be often but not overwhelming, weekly at the most, monthly at the least. Mailing out material often is expensive, so electronic means are preferred. This should be your largest group in your contact list and you should be adding people to it all the time. Avoid general invitations like, "Join us some Sunday," and instead keep invitations specific: "Join us this Saturday for…" Specific invitations to specific events are far more effective. You want to be added to their calendar. And always remember to relate it to your why!

Interested

These are people who you determine are interested in your community and connecting to your why. It's a judgement call when folks move from prospect to interested. Regular communication is important with this group and it should have a more personal touch since it's a smaller group of people. Invitation made through individual emails, handwritten notes, and personal phone calls are key. This is the group you will spend the most time on. As they connect with your why they need to start connecting with you as people. In the beginning most people don't mind being anonymous in the crowd. Over time, though, people want others to know their name, learn about them, and miss them when they are gone. People are more likely to show up and participate if they personally know others who will be there.

You still need to reinforce your why with this group and they should continue to receive what you send the prospect group. Do not take this group for granted and do not assume they will simply find their own way in your community. They will need guides to help them in the first part of their journey with you.

Involved

The involved group are those people who you expect to show up fairly regularly, with the understanding that the definition of "regular" is shifting. Those newer to church feel they are doing a good job if they make it to worship once a month. It's also not uncommon for people to be much more committed to a small group, mission team, or other project before they become committed to regular worship attendance. You need to take all of this into account when you determine who is "involved."

The involved group still will need reminders of your why, but they also need to know when things are happening. They can tolerate more information about the administrative side of the church. Some will even expect it. These folks are becoming insiders and they need to be treated as not just receivers of services from your church but partners.

The challenge here is to not go so far that you are overloading them with meeting minutes and dry finance updates. Remember they are with you for a reason and you will need to remind them of that reason. It's important to check in with this group to get their feedback about how they are growing and where the church is, or isn't, helping them grow. This can give you valuable insights into your strengths and opportunities for growth.

Leader

Leaders are those who are shaping the culture of your church. These aren't people who sit on committees. There is a difference. Leaders in your church are the ones who people listen to. The ones who set the tone.

Communicating with these folks can be challenging. They are leaders because they are comfortable with you and have a strong routine of involvement. They likely don't think much about the why of church and have their own reasons for being involved. Winning over leaders is a key in making your why more broadly known and shared. This is likely a small group and communication looks like one-on-one or small group conversations with other leaders. They are respected and they will respond best to others they considered respected.

It is not the goal that everyone become a leader in your church. For many, they will express their faith and gifts in other ways. You also may be nurturing people who will become leaders in other places like local nonprofits, schools, or civic organizations. These leaders should be celebrated and affirmed just as much as leaders in your congregation. After all, they are all working to show God's grace and love, just in different ways.

It is as important to communicate your why to the leaders as it is the prospects and can be almost as difficult to get through to them. Instead of talking at them, consider soliciting their advice. Make them part of the effort so they feel valued. With leaders it is critical to listen more than you talk so they feel heard. Even if they disagree with you, things will go much better if they feel heard.

Intentional Invitation

Good communication won't happen by accident and can't be left to chance. In the beginning you can get away with being a bit haphazard, but as things progress you will outgrow working that way quickly.

You need a communication and outreach plan and to prepare for things well in advance.

Churches often go to great efforts to plan an event then spend almost no time inviting people to it. I've been guilty of it myself more than once. We still assume an announcement at worship or a line in the newsletter is sufficient. It isn't. And it certainly isn't if your goal is to reach people outside of your church. Adding "please invite your friends" isn't much help either. If you are planning an event, you need to spend a good amount of time and energy on your invitation strategy even if it means planning something less complicated so you have the time and resources to spend on it.

Invitation is key to any evangelism strategy, yet most of us rarely do it. Invitation can feel scary to many people. We don't want to bother people and, perhaps more importantly, we don't want to be rejected. But really the worst case is someone says no. In the overall scheme of life that's not that bad.

Practicing invitation takes intention. It's a muscle that must be exercised and strengthened. Once you've developed the muscle it becomes second nature. I was once attending a conference in England with a couple church planters I work with. At one pub we struck up a conversation with our server. He intended to visit the United States soon and one of my planters jumped on it. He wasn't planning to be even in the same state as her but she invited him to her new church plant anyway and gave him a card. She's an inviting machine!

We all won't go that far, but we can all be better. All it takes is the will to do it, someone to invite, and something to invite them to. The first part is just a matter choice; the second two take energy and planning. At a church I served we had a trunk-or-treat event that hosted hundreds of kids on Halloween. After a couple years of doing it I noticed we were missing an opportunity. Here all these people were, in our parking lot, and nobody was inviting them to church! So the following year we scheduled a special kid-focused worship service for the Sunday following Halloween. We put our puppet ministry front and center in the service and we printed cards advertising the service. I then set up a puppet screen in the back of our family's van and interacted with the kids as they came by as my puppet alter ego, Peep. Peep told silly jokes and invited every kid to the service. Another volunteer slipped a card in each kid's bag with the candy.

It's critical to create specific opportunities for you to make invitations. I'm not a big fan of chatting up people in line at Starbucks. I also don't think that works very well. But when you have groups in your building, that is an opportunity. Also look for public places your church can be. My favorite example of this is a local church in my area that rents a booth at the local fair each summer and offers it as a baby changing area. They staff it with friendly people who interact with parents when they stop in. I'm sure they are being invited to church. Other churches have had booths at the farmers' market, handed out water during parades, street fairs, or marches. Wherever people gather you can be there with an offering of grace and a warm invitation.

There is a common false assumption that many of us suffer from. The assumption is that if people are in our building as part of a group or for an event they'll eventually check us out on Sunday morning. The corollary is the assumption that if people encounter you in the community on a service project in a church T-shirt they'll magically show up to worship. While you may luck into a couple of folks this way this isn't something you should count on. The nones and the dones either have no interest or no idea what your church does or why they should care. You are just that place where their kid attends scouts or they go for a free meal. If you want to be more than that to them it is your job to educate them. Yours and nobody else's. It is perfectly reasonable when a group uses your space to ask that someone from your church be allowed to offer a welcome. That welcome should talk about who you are and why you do what you do. It can go something like this:

Welcome to our church. We are so glad you are with us. Here we believe our faith requires us to serve our community and welcoming you as our partners is part of that calling. If you have any questions about our church, please feel free to ask me. Also, if you are passionate like we are about this community please consider checking out SOME EVENT. If you want more information about that please let me know. God bless each of you and the work of this group.

Get Their Name

Names are critical to everything discussed thus far. If you don't know someone's name, you can't build relationships. If you aren't putting yourself in a position to learn new names, you are not doing evangelism. One of the most important jobs you can assign someone is to learn names. Many churches pass around attendance pads during worship; that's a start. But that can't be all you do. You can't put someone in your prospect pool if you don't know their name and how to contact them.

When you are out in the community or hosting events for the neighborhood at your church you need to learn people's names. To do this, obviously, you have to be in the same space as them, interacting with them, and generally being hospitable. A big pet peeve for me is when churches host community meals or events and the church people are all in the kitchen or at one table together and not interacting with anyone else there.

I was working with the pastor of a church which started a community garden program. They invited their neighbors to have garden plots in raised beds they constructed on their property. Several community people took them up on it and they spent the summer weeding and watering on the church grounds. After the first year the church realized that while their neighbors had physically been in their space no new relationships were forming. People were working at different times and on different days so rarely did people get a chance to meet. The next year they planned a fall harvest dinner where participants were encouraged to come, share the food they had grown, and get to know one another. When I asked the pastor how that went he looked a bit sheepish. Apparently the community members had a good time, mingled, and formed new connections. The church people, on the other hand, sat by themselves and didn't learn any new names. What a missed opportunity!

There is a gravitational pull we feel toward people we already know that only gets stronger the more a room is populated with people we do not know. This is why we must be intentional about stepping outside of our comfort zone when the opportunity is given. Being intentional doesn't need to be overly difficult. The pastor in the story above just needed to give the following instructions to his members before the dinner:

- Learn the names of three new people.
- Get one person's email address.

Even the second one doesn't need to be that difficult. Before the event, talk over how what you are doing relates to your why. Make sure everyone can give a short thirty-second talk about the event and your church why. Then use that talk while you are meeting new folks. If someone seems interested in what you said, ask for their email so you can send them more information. Because email is so easy to ignore most people are more comfortable giving out their email address than their home address or phone number.

For the event above, the thirty-second talk might go like this:

We are very excited to host the community garden. This church really believes in the sustainability of growing our own local food rather than shipping it in from great distances. I believe it is more in line with how God asks us to care for the planet and use its resources well. That is part of what makes me a proud member of this place. This is just one of the many things we do.

It is just that easy. Though you may want to practice a few times before. Like many things this will feel awkward at first. But in no time you will get comfortable with it. It just takes willingness to try and practice.

I hope that you see intention is the key to everything. Nothing will happen by accident. And yes, this takes time and energy. It also begins to generate its own energy quickly. Being a witness isn't meant to be a drag; it's meant to be life giving. Learning to take time and see God at work means we get to more fully experience the Holy Spirit. Learning your why, the deeper thing you are trying to live out, gives you clarity of purpose. Sharing what God is doing and the why of your church and life with others gives you an opportunity to connect on a deeper level than just talking about the weather. All of these things feed the soul and you will learn quickly that they give life, not drain it.

Get to Work

How is your team praying? Are you taking time to invite the Holy Spirit into your time? Try praying the news or Lectio Divina if you haven't done so already. Challenge people to pray in some way each day for the next two weeks. Consider setting a daily reminder on your phone.

How will you pray daily for the next two weeks?

How will you remind yourself of this commitment?

Review the levels of involvement (Prospect, Interested, Committed, Leader). How will your church track people and their stage of involvement?

For each level what is your communication strategy? What will you use to communicate with them and how often? Consider all the ways you can communicate: email, Facebook, Twitter, text, phone call, newsletter. Consider you need a mix of bulk communication and individual communication especially for *interested* and *leader*.

Prospect

Interested

Committed

Leader

One-on-ones

How many one-on-ones and by when? Every team member needs a goal for this. Also, how many referrals will you strive for? That is the most important measure.

In pairs practice having a one-on-one conversation. May sure you are able to share the why of your church sometime during the conversation. Also make sure you leave with a better understanding of the why of the person you are talking with.

6. Show up

John 2:1-11

On the third day there was a wedding in Cana of Galilee, and the mother of Jesus was there. Jesus and his disciples had also been invited to the wedding. When the wine gave out, the mother of Jesus said to him, "They have no wine." And Jesus said to her, "Woman, what concern is that to you and to me? My hour has not yet come." His mother said to the servants, "Do whatever he tells you." Now standing there were six stone water jars for the Jewish rites of purification, each holding twenty or thirty gallons. Jesus said to them, "Fill the jars with water." And they filled them up to the brim. He said to them, "Now draw some out, and take it to the chief steward." So they took it. When the steward tasted the water that had become wine, and did not know where it came from (though the servants who had drawn the water knew), the steward called the bridegroom and said to him, "Everyone serves the good wine first, and then the inferior wine after the guests have become drunk. But you have kept the good wine until now." Jesus did this, the first of his signs, in Cana of Galilee, and revealed his glory; and his disciples believed in him.

The truth is, chatting people up while you are in line at Starbucks is awkward and cold calling by knocking on doors rates just above root canals for most people. And, as a bonus, they aren't that effective. Now for some people in some places cold calling does work and I'm by no means against it. I also know that if that is the only option most people will choose to do nothing instead. Thankfully there are other options that are less frightening and oftentimes more effective. They are: *join a group, crash a party,* and *throw a party.* We'll go through each one in a moment but first we need to remember our why.

Nothing we are about to discuss will do you any good unless you first know your why. Previously you were asked to come up with a thirty second or less talk about your why, something you can have committed to memory and available whenever you need it. It needs to be compelling to non-church folk, people based, and memorable. You need this for a couple of reasons. First, you need it for you and your community. You need to be able to remind yourself who you are and have something at the ready when hard choices need to be made. When you are tempted to bicker over small things or divide into factions over the color of the carpet, your why reminds you of your larger purpose and helps keep you united. Some churches form their why into a unison prayer they use at the start of all meetings.

The other reason you need to have your why close at hand is at some point someone is going to ask you about your church and you better have an answer more compelling than, "It's a bunch of nice people." Nice people are everywhere. What you want instead is to be able to share your church's why and see if that sparks interest in the other person. If it does then you've opened a door to share more. This is where having stories about how your church lives out its why is important. Actually, more than important, it's critical. Stories are how information spreads among people. Long before it was written down the Bible was a collection of stories shared, person to person, for centuries. Stories matter so much that the author Seth Godin states emphatically in his book *All Marketers are Liars*, "Either you're going to tell stories that spread, or you will become irrelevant."[12] You must be prepared with stories that bring your why to life through real, relatable examples.

Finally you need to have an invitation at the ready. Some specific opportunity you can invite people to be a part of, like the children's focused service the Sunday after trunk-or-treat on Halloween. The key is specific. Not, "Check us out on Sunday sometime." That's too vague. You need something that happens at

---

[12] *All Marketers are Liars* by Seth Godin, 2009, Pg. 1

a specific time and place that is a good representation of who you are as a church. It may be a worship service or it may be a volunteer opportunity or an event you are throwing for the community. Whatever it is, you should have it at the ready.

Now, some of you are objecting that this all feels too calculated and manipulative. I understand that. However, if you think about it, this really is what we do naturally all the time. If someone asks you about what you are wearing, you'll tell them where you got it. If it's a place you enjoy shopping, you'll naturally tell them that, too, saying something like, "I love it there because they have a great selection and the staff doesn't bother you trying to be overly helpful." When you do that you are telling them your why for why you shop a particular place. If it sparks interest, you'll likely follow it up with a story about a great deal you got last Saturday. If it's going well, you may even point out they have a great sale coming up next weekend and ask them to go with you.

We do this by nature for stores and products we love, for movies and other entertainment, and for groups or social organizations we are a part of. If you volunteer at Habitat for Humanity every month, you have a better reason for it than, "I like to swing hammers." And I bet you can share that why off the cuff in a compelling way on demand. Further, I'd bet you do share it when given the chance.

So, why can't we do this for the church?

For most of us the reason is that we simply just never think about it. That has to change. With a little intention and practice we can be as effective sharing our why of church as we are our why of Kohl's, Costco, or the local food bank.

Join a Group

Now that you've delved deep into sharing your why the question is, where do you share it? We'll talk about three ways: first by joining a group. Small towns and large cities all have organizations that live inside of them. Some are very formal and others haphazard. The neighborhood my previous church was part of had a task force set up by the city. Each neighborhood had one and when things happened that affected our area the task force would be asked to give an opinion on what to do. It also met with representatives from the police and fire departments to hear about concerns they saw in the area. The task force had no real authority other than to convene a conversation and give an opinion, yet people attended. I started to attend about a year into my ministry and was the only person representing a church at the meetings. Attending gave me the inside track on what was going on in our neighborhood, what the needs were, and the ability to offer ourselves as a resource when needed. It also gave me the chance to talk about the church and what we were doing.

Joining a group (or several) is a slow-burn process. You may not see fruit from it for quite a while and that's fine. Be patient. It will, however, give you opportunities to share your why and build new relationships if you do it right. It's not enough to attend and simply introduce yourself as so-and-so from such-and-such church and leave it at that. You'll need to find opportunities to interject your why, which are far more common than people assume. If you are asked casually, "How is it going?" the door has been cracked open. Share a short anecdote about your church that demonstrates your why. I always had a free store story at the ready. If someone seems interested then share more. Our church's why was related to Matthew 25, so if the free store caught people's attention I would follow up with something like, "Our church believes when Jesus said feed the hungry, clothe the naked, and visit the prisoner he meant it. So we strive to equip people to make a difference in our neighborhood." If that sparks more interest, I would follow up with, "The free store is open next Saturday and we have a lot of new donations to sort. We could really use some help if you are interested."

Done, easy as that. At more formal group meetings these opportunities happen around the edges before or after the program, usually near the coffeepot. Look for them and you'll find them.

In most communities there are also less formal groups without names or agendas. I don't know how many of the men at my last church were part of some sort of regular coffee group. They'd meet at all sorts of places at a regular time and just chat. Nobody officially organized the group; it just manifested over time. Similarly there is a group of car enthusiasts who gather at a local fast-food place Thursday nights. Why? Who knows! But they are there.

Formal or informal, joining a group is a long-term evangelism strategy that should not be ignored. You don't have to organize the group or lead it. Just show up with a story ready to share and be prepared to listen to the stories of others.

Crash a Party

There are all sorts of events that happen regularly in towns big and small on a regular basis. Weekend farmers' markets, county fairs, and marches or demonstrations are happening all around you. Some are more appropriate for some churches than others. This, again, is where your why will serve you. What is happening in your community that fits with your why? If you are a church focused on music, what could fit with that? If you are a justice-seeking church, where do other justice seekers gather? If you are a dinner church, where do people go who care about quality food? Crashing a party is about letting others do the work of gathering people together so that you can show up and be part.

Any place that provides booth space is a good opportunity. You could do something as simple as hand out water if it's a hot day. Other churches have brought in licensed massage therapists for chair massage or volunteer hairstylists for free back-to-school cuts at community events aimed at those living on the margins. Another church makes and sells bread at the weekly farmers' market for both outreach and fundraising. The options really are limitless.

It also doesn't have to be as involved as staffing a booth; you can also just show up and meet people. Just remember that is why you are there. One way to keep focus at events is to count how many people you talk to. Not every conversation will be fruitful; that's fine. But you won't get to the fruitful ones if you don't start conversations. Like one-on-ones, this is a community organizing basic strategy. In fact, a good outcome of crashing a party is one or more follow-up one-on-ones. So measure your success by how many conversations you have with new people and how many follow-up one-on-ones you arrange.

Many churches already have practices that put them out into the community as part of different events. The church I grew up in had a pie-selling booth at the county fair going back decades. It raised some money, which is good, but I don't think ever raised awareness of the church, which is not so good. Part of the issue is that it's a big leap from pie to Jesus. Sure, people love pie, and Jesus loves everyone, but it sort of breaks down after that. Also, in those days, churches didn't really worry about their why because the standard assumption was that people already knew why churches existed. What you really wanted to do was show that you had the best pie at your church! Well, in a world with more and more nones and dones those assumptions won't cut it.

So what do we do with the pie stand? Tear it

down? Not so fast. First, consider your shoes. TOMS shoes is a newcomer to the footwear world but is taking it by storm. Not because they have a better shoe. I know because I own a pair and they are a good shoe but nothing stellar. What makes TOMS different is their mission. For each shoe they sell they make sure a child who needs shoes somewhere in the world gets a pair. Their mission—providing footwear to the underserved—has made something as boring as buying shoes exciting. When I bought mine, I ended up telling the cashier and the person behind me in line why I was so excited about these otherwise normal shoes!

So, back to the pie. What does selling it support? If it goes to your mission's fund, great! How can you let everyone know that each piece of pie equals one donation to the local food bank? If the proceeds go to your church power bill that's fine, too. What does that bill support? Does AA use your building? Do you have a youth group that gives children in your community a place to be themselves and escape the pressures of a constantly connected life? How does the pie support your why and how can you share that story? That is the missing piece you need to add.

Urban Coffee in Dallas, Texas is a new church start that looks just like a normal coffee shop, because it is. Which means regular people come in off the street all the time to buy their coffee. One thing Urban Coffee does is donate ten percent of the proceeds of all sales to a local cause. So when you buy a latte the sale ends with, "Thank you for supporting children's literacy today." (Or whatever the cause is.) Every sale, every time. And if people ask about it, they get the twenty-second version of Urban Coffee's why about how they believe in building a better world by developing new leaders. You can easily do the same with pie, or thrift stores, or whatever. It just takes intention.

When you crash a party what you want to bring with you is your why and make sure you have a way to share it. The pastor shouldn't be the only one with church business cards. Anyone who is going to join a group or crash a party should have some. That way you are prepared to invite people to follow up with you.

Crashing a party can be a big production or a small one. Sometimes it will lead to several new connections and one-on-ones; sometimes it will be a dud. Either way is fine. The strikeouts are part of playing the game and the cost you pay for a chance at a home run. The more parties you crash, the easier it will become for you to make them fruitful.

Throw a Party

Sometimes there simply is no group to join or party to crash where the people you want to reach are gathered. That is when you many need to consider throwing your own party. In most churches this is our default, which I why I list the other two first. Throwing a party the right way is a lot of work. If what you are after is opportunities to meet people, it's easier to go where they are already gathered. But if that is not an option then you may need to do your own thing.

The most important starting place for your event is, you guessed it, your why. Whatever you do needs to relate somehow to the why of your church. You'll need to make a connection between the event and your why if you want to spark interest in your church with new people. As the pie demonstrates above, you have a lot of room to work with; the closer related the two are, the better.

The trunk-or-treat mentioned before is an example of throwing a party. On another occasion we hosted a chili cook off between churches as a fundraiser for the free store. Scout Sunday was always big, especially if we were handing out awards to our local scouts. This brought lots of new families to worship.

The logistics of actually throwing an event can be as complicated or as easy as you want. Trunk-or-treat is simple, as is a parking lot barbeque. The difficult part is not getting so wrapped up in the logistics that you forget the marketing. After all, why throw a party if you aren't going to invite anyone? Marketing your event should be where you spend most of your time. You are better off planning a simpler event if it means you have more time for marketing.

With a CLVI[13] license churches can show major studio movies in their church. I have heard of

---

[13] Visit http://us.cvli.com. Please be aware of the restrictions around showing movies publically. If in doubt give them a call; they are very helpful.

churches that do "drive-in" night in their parking lot with a simple projector and PA system. People bring lawn chairs and pop popcorn. Before the movie starts they plan "previews" of upcoming happenings at the church filmed on someone's iPhone that include a specific invitation to some upcoming event.

Getting the word out requires several things in today's information-saturated world. If you want to cut through the noise, you have to be different. People are amazing at tuning out things they see all the time. Instead, what catches our attention is change. Here are some ways to get the word out about your party.

Banners

If you have a building on a street with even mild traffic, banners are cheap and effective. They are temporary so they tend to get noticed, which is good. There are also lots of places to buy them online. The trick with banners is to first make sure that people can actually see them. Drive down your street and figure out the best placement of the banner before you hang it. Put yourself where the public is and make sure it is visible. Second, don't put too much information on it. For our trunk-or-treat the banner reads, "Trunk-or-Treat, Free Candy and Hot Drinks, 5-7pm" in large, high-contrast letters.

Online

Every party needs a Facebook event with pictures on your church Facebook page. You may even consider doing a "boosted" event where you pay

Facebook a small fee to promote your event in the feed of people near your location. This is far cheaper and more effective than ads in the paper. Also, make sure as many people as possible in your church are trained to share your events on Facebook. Ask them during worship, "We all shared the upcoming back-to-school bash on Facebook, right?" Finally, look at places like NextDoor.com and other networking sites. I have heard stories from several people that a well-worded post on NextDoor is the most helpful thing they've done.

Door Hangers

Printed door hangers are proven to be more effective than direct mail, though neither is all that effective. Door hangers save you the cost of postage and can be distributed by various groups in your church. Ideally you would encourage small teams to do a prayer walk while they are distributing, praying for the houses and people they encounter along the way. This is a great activity for youth and children's ministries.

Back in 1964 Marshall McLuhan coined the phrase, "The medium is the message,"[14] meaning that how you say something is more important than what you say. You will communicate more about yourself and your church by *how* you communicate than what you say with your words. If your banners are ugly,

---

[14] https://en.wikipedia.org/wiki/The_medium_is_the_message

nobody will notice the words. If you Facebook event doesn't have a compelling cover photo, nobody will read the description. If your door hangers are sloppy, they'll go straight in the trash. The best investment you can make is to ensure that all your marketing materials look good. We are in a time when good design trumps all. Apple products aren't coveted just because they perform well. They are coveted because they are beautiful.

Nobody Knows Nobody

The first house my wife and I bought was in a brand-new development in Albuquerque, New Mexico. We were the second-to-last house built on our cul-de-sac and our final neighbors joined a few months later. Though the houses were built close together we never really got to know our neighbors. Finally we encountered the newest neighbors at the communal mailbox and they took the initiative to invite us over for tea. He was from Scotland and she was from Mexico. As we talked our neighbor lamented that at first he was excited to have a garage to park in but then soon realized that because of it he wasn't able to get to know his neighbors. He was keying into the fact that our cars, garages, and smartphones are all great, but they are also isolating us. We simply don't have as many opportunities to interact with people we happen to meet.

Recently I was on a check-in call with several of my church planters. I was asking them what their plans for the Lenten season were and one of my planters shared something rather profound. They had discovered among their leadership that few people involved in the church had regular interaction with folks outside of the church. "Nobody knows anybody anymore," he shared. So their Lenten practice was to temporarily disband their adult Bible study and encourage people to spend that time participating in a group or event outside of the church. Brilliant! They gave people back some time and asked them to invest it in forming new connections with the wider community. What could be better? What would it look like in your church to suspend a group or activity even for a month and invite people to instead be in the neighborhood meeting new people in new ways?

In the passage that opens this chapter Jesus performs his first miracle in the Gospel of John while he's at a party. At first Jesus is hesitant because it is a public space and he doesn't feel ready. We all feel this way. But his mother is a good mother and leaves him to make a choice. We have the same choice. We can think we are unprepared to share in public places. It's easy to fall back on small talk about the weather or the latest news. That feels more comfortable for many. But what happens if we are never willing to be brave? What happens if Jesus doesn't turn the water into wine? What happens if Jesus' public ministry never begins? What happens if nobody from your church ever shares with people outside your church? Neither scenario is good.

So find opportunities to share your why and the

stories of your church. God wants love to be shared, not contained, and that is why you do evangelism. So stop worrying, get out there, and try. The God of the universe is rooting for you.

Get to Work

We are deep into the practical things now, and you may be starting to feel a little overwhelmed; that's normal. It will take months to get up to speed on everything presented in this book. So be gentle with yourself and give yourself some grace.

This chapter is all about being present. In church speak we call this being incarnational. The defining claim for Christianity is that God actually became a person to be with us. Proclamations from burning bushes, various prophets, and stone tablets weren't getting the job done. So, as scripture says, *And the Word became flesh and lived among us.*[15] It is the same for us. To make God known in places where fewer and fewer people know God, we have to show up. We have to be incarnational like Christ was and show up in people's lives in all the ways we can.

So what groups are you going to join? What are going to stop doing so you can participate in that community? How will you bring your why?

What parties can your church crash? How will you find parties to be a part of? How will you bring your why with you?

What parties will you throw? How will you invite people? How will you connect them to your why?

---

[15] John 1:14 NRSV.

Groups I will join.

Parties I will crash.

Parties we will throw.

I will caution you again about throwing too many parties. It's better to do less and do it better. Meaning, spend less time throwing a high quantity of events and make sure you put the time into the invitation and outreach.

What are some invitation strategies you might employ?

7. Get them talking

Word of mouth is the best advertising there is. It's a cliché because it is true. This whole book focuses on relationships because relationships are the strongest bridge to build on. People naturally assume that paid spokespeople are exaggerating and that advertisements lie. At the same time, we assume our friends and family are being truthful and forthright. So when we see or hear the advertisement telling us the new restaurant in town is great, we largely ignore it. When a friend or even an acquaintance tells us the same thing, we listen.

The most important thing you can do is get people talking about your church. People don't often repeat facts and figures they encounter, but they do repeat stories. Jonah Berger in his book *Contagious: Why*

Things Catch On[16] shares six principles for why things catch on and are shared:

- Social Currency
- Triggers
- Emotion
- Public
- Practical Value
- Stories

Let's look at each of these briefly. Social currency is the recognition that we share things that make us look good. If we get a good deal at a store, we share it because it makes us look smart. On the other hand, if we burn dinner, we don't typically share it as widely because it makes us look bad. The lesson for the church is that if people don't feel good about their association with the church, why would they ever share about the church? Internal evangelism—helping people understand the good they are a part of—is critical to any external evangelism strategy. You need to be reminding people often about the good work they are a part of by being part of your church. And remind them often!

We are constantly surrounded by triggers: images, smells, and sounds that cause us to remember something from sometime else. To this day the plastic smell of freshly opened brand-new electronics reminds me of connecting my first Nintendo

---

[16] Jonah Berger, *Contagious: Why Things Catch On*, 2013, p. 207.

Entertainment System when I was eleven years old. I'm instantly back in that basement guiding Mario on his adventure every time I smell it. Sermons focused on real-world themes and metaphors can provide a triggering effect. Branded coffee mugs that sit on members' desks at work can do the same. Text reminders during the week can be intentional triggers if they fit with a theme and they can create an opportunity to share with others.

Emotion is something we find all over scripture. One reason the stories of the Bible are so memorable is that they make us feel. If something is dull, it won't get shared. But if something makes us feel happy, joyful, encouraged, or even angry, it is way more likely to be passed around. Just look at your Facebook feed or latest viral YouTube video to see what I mean. Emotion works on us all.

Public means that it's able to be seen and shared. When everything your church does is locked inside the building no one can see it, and that's not helpful. A church I served had one service every summer that took place outside in the parking lot. Partly because it was a fun break from the norm. But mostly so that when people drove by they would see us and know there was life here. I always put the rented giant inflatable slide as close to the road as we safely could. It publicly shouted to the world, "We love kids."

Practical value is the complement to emotion. While facts and figures rarely go viral, we do care and share about things that make our life better. Think back to chapter three and the six categories from the

How We Gather study: Community, Personal Transformation, Social Transformation, Purpose Finding, Creativity, and Accountability. These categories are the practical values people get out of the communities in the study. Helping people understand how they are better people and how the neighborhood is improved through you church helps them better understand and share they value they receive.

Finally, stories are what most of this book is about. Stories capture meaning and wrap it up in a way that is easy to share. You can recite facts and figures all you want but they won't stick with people the way stories will. They also can't be as easily shared. Tell the stories of the lives your church touches and the ways your community is being transformed. Don't tell me about the 150 people you feed at your community meal; tell me about the family you served that has no other place to sit and eat together because they are living in a cheap motel. That I will remember.

As you share about your church through various means it's important to keep the six principles above in mind. Not everything you do will check all six boxes and that's fine. However, looking at these six it's easy to understand why your monthly newsletter with the dates for the next church council meeting featured boldly on the cover isn't getting much traction. Perhaps there is some practical value for those in your church announcing that, but not for anyone else. It's also no wonder why things like pictures are so important, too. A picture can communicate emotions, trigger memories, and tell a story far better than even a thousand well-chosen words can.

There are some basic strategies for communicating both internally and externally that should be practiced at all churches.

Online Strategy

You can no longer ignore the internet; it's not going anywhere. What's important is to know which platform to use for what. Let's start with two: your website and Facebook. Every church needs a website and an active Facebook page. Your website tells people all the more permanent information about your church. People should be able to find easily your location, worship times, basic biographies of your pastor and staff, and some understanding of your why. A welcome video by your pastor and a key layperson would go a long way, too. Too often churches fail to update their websites regularly, so keep it to things that don't change that often.

Facebook is where the daily life of your church should be found, and a link to your Facebook page should be easily findable on your website. Churches should have updates on their page at least three times a week with a focus on pictures and short stories. This is not the time to write in paragraphs; a few sentences will do. Let the pictures speak for you. Events coming up should be listed and church members need to be actively encouraged to click "attending" on posted events. It may not be news to you that members who show up to everything are planning to be there, but it may be news to their Facebook friends. When a person clicks "like" or "attending" on an event or other post it increases the likelihood Facebook will show that event or post to a person's friend. Facebook is always trying to show you things you might be interested in, and if your friend is interested in something, it's likely you are, too.

Learning to use these two tools well at a basic level is critical. Once you've got the basics down there are some more options.

Advanced Online

Chances are your church is already listed on Google Maps and Yelp.com. Both of these sites not only give you directions to various locations like stores, restaurants, and museums, they also allow normal people to leave reviews of all these places, including your church. Search Engine Optimization or SEO is the art to influencing these platforms. The easiest thing to do is to recruit different members of your church to write five-star reviews. If you Google "best church in *your town*," the first listing will be a map with churches with high reviews listed first. Typically there are not many total reviews for churches so even a few extra positive reviews are helpful. Nothing may ever come of it, but for a very low investment in time it's worth doing.

Producing video of reasonable quality is now available to anyone with a newer smartphone. The cameras have gotten so good even major directors are experimenting with using them in regular filmmaking. Each week you work to put a quality worship experience together around a theme. Why not record a short video sharing that week's theme and an invitation to worship? No need to get fancy, just stand somewhere attractive and record. Keep it to thirty seconds or less; people want you to get to the point. Post it to Facebook with something like, "I am so excited for this Sunday where we will be talking about *whatever*. Please join us Sunday at ten a.m. at *your church*." Digital recording means you are not wasting film if it takes you a couple tries. So if you don't do it around thirty seconds the first time, just do it again!

Another option is to offer a similar thirty-second video on Monday reminding people about the theme from Sunday and invite them into further consideration of what you presented. This can be filmed at the same time on Thursday and then use Facebook's schedule post feature for the following Monday. You may also want a midweek post that simply reminds people you are praying for them and ask if there is anything that you can pray about for them. Again, you can schedule all this ahead of time. You now have three quality touch points each week through Facebook that take less than an hour to set up once a week!

Soft Evangelism

Churches, like any other organization or product, need branding. A logo for your church that is consistent across your sign, website, Facebook page, newsletter, etc. is critical. A well-designed logo is a trigger for your church and, hopefully, will remind people of something pleasant. Having a logo opens you up to additional *soft evangelism* opportunities. Stickers on your cars, embroidered shirts and hats, and T-Shirts are all good opportunities to get your name out into the world. Jerry Herships, a church planter in the Denver Area, loves to put stickers for his faith community *After Hours* in random places. He often posts on Facebook pictures of new and interesting places he's found to put a sticker.

If your church does regular volunteer work in the community, consider printed T-shirts with your church name on them. When you crash a party or attend a group it's good to somehow advertise who you are. You never know, it may start a conversation where you can share your why!

Calendar

A colleague of mine has one wall in her office covered in a giant dry erase calendar. I'm partial to digital calendars myself, but this is rather brilliant. At a glance she can see exactly what she's up to in the near and distant future. One of the big challenges about intentional evangelism is not letting things creep up on you because that's when we get into trouble. Our great plans to market an event go out the window when we realize it's right around the corner.

Creating a visible central calendar will remind you of important things coming up and give you a visual reference for the activity level of your church. Are you too busy, not giving yourself time to do things well? Are you not busy enough? Are all your activities just for your members or is the community involved? Here you may want to color code: green for church-focused events and red for community. Perhaps blue for special events you want to market to your neighborhood. Are there monthly blue events?

Bringing it all Together

Back at the start of this book we talked about how evangelism isn't about growing your church or getting more people to worship to put money in the plate. That may happen, and if it does, great, but that's not the point. The point is the recognition that there is a God of love in the universe and that our job is to introduce people to that God. To do that first we must recognize God when we encounter what God is up to in our lives and neighborhoods, which can be more difficult than it sounds for a church that is out of practice.

A life of faith is not always an easy one. Faith puts demands on you and causes you to think of others before yourself. But faith is never a simply a burden to be borne or a duty to fulfill. Faith is about connecting yourself to the source of all the good in the world and allowing yourself to be an instrument of that good. Evangelism, then, shouldn't simply drain us of time and energy. If it does, you are doing it wrong. If you aren't throwing parties you yourself wouldn't want to attend, they probably aren't worth throwing. Instead, evangelism should become a source of energy as God's love is noticed and proclaimed. Our job, after all, is to tell people they are loved! What could be better than that?

So do not fear or put off your outreach into the community. If you are worried about the future of your church, as many are, take that energy and direct it toward your neighborhood. Help them see the love that is all around us and witness it yourself while you are at it. If you need hope then share hope. If you need peace then share peace. If you crave love then show love. This is how God intended the world to work. Lose your life for God and you will gain more than you imagined. That is what being a follower of Jesus is all about.

Get to Work

It's time to put everything you have learned together. I hope at this point you are feeling excited; that's good! Ready to take on the world? Great! Now just one thing: slow down. The old adage is true: slow down to go faster. Figure out what comes next for you and then what comes after that. Celebrate all the small successes along the way because that is what will give you energy for the weeks and months to come.

You need an overall strategy that should cover at least the next twelve months. It should include:

- Developing and sharing your why
- Looking at your marketing materials like your logo, website, Facebook page, and business cards
- Developing a strategy for one-on-ones
- Developing a way to track and categorize people you encounter
- Building your calendar
- Joining groups
- Crashing parties
- Throwing parties

For each you will need to identify the tasks to be accomplished, who will do it, and by when. This could be a large list to start and you should spend at least a year. You also need to schedule regular check-ins on progress. Currently I hope you are excited, but that excitement will fade. Keep moving forward even when you feel less motivated. This is long-term work and in the end it will pay off.

Always remember that you are a beloved child of God. Never lose sight of that. Remember why you are doing this in the first place.

You will receive power when the Holy Spirit has come upon you, and you will be my witnesses in Jerusalem, in all Judea and Samaria, and to the end of the earth.

-Jesus

Appendix: Notes on Preaching

In chapter four we talked about the need to celebrate and the opportunity presented in worship to invite people into celebrating with us. The preaching moment is often one of the best opportunities for doing this. The days of the three-point sermon as the standard model of preaching are behind us. People are looking for inspiration more than information today. This is doubly true for the nones and dones. The sermon is your chance to remind people they are God's children. Glide Memorial Church goes so far as to call their Sunday morning experience a "Celebration." You won't find the word worship anywhere on their sign or website. So preach the good news as good news and remind people that the news is indeed good!

Listen to Others

One of the best habits any regular preacher can have is to listen to other preachers. Chefs are constantly watching and learning from other chefs to learn new techniques and flavor combinations. Hairstylists, artists, and designers also learn from each other constantly. Given the number of churches that stream, podcast, and post their services to YouTube, there is no lack of opportunity. Every preacher should have at least two other preachers they listen to regularly.

Connect the Dots

The preaching time is your chance to connect the dots for people. To me the free store was an obvious expression of the why of our church, but I constantly encountered regular attenders who didn't understand that. Philosopher Alain de Botton in his TED talk *Atheism 2.0*[17] argues that one strength of the church is that we repeat a consistent message each Sunday. He argues that in the world of academic philosophy they assume reading Plato once is sufficient to make a lasting impact. Any behavior scientist or parent of small children will tell you that you have to repeat things if you want them to stick. I'm not sure Alain has been to many churches recently because I'm constantly having conversations with pastors who assume that just because they said something once in a sermon people should get it. My experience is that once is never enough.

As you prepare your weekly message you should be reviewing the why of your church and asking yourself, "Does what I am preparing today help us live out our why?" If not then you need to ask yourself why you are planning to share it.

Some congregations take their why and turn it into a regular prayer or commissioning statement at the end of each service, something that people can

---

[17] See www.ted.com/talks/alain_de_botton_atheism_2_0.

memorize over time so that it becomes part of the heart language of the church.

Tell the Right Stories

I am a storytelling preacher. I like to tell stories when I preach. Sometimes they are stories I read online, found on Facebook, or from my life. I have noticed, though, that the stories that stick, the ones people really pay attention to, are stories from the church community I am speaking to. These days I guest preach and I usually ask my host if there is some story of their church they would like me to highlight. This creates what worship consultant Jason Moore calls "the lean-in effect." People like to hear about themselves and where God is working in your church. As we help people learn how to celebrate it can be helpful to share examples from outside your church; it is actually far more effective to use stories from inside your church.

Sermon Quick Test

As you prepare your message ask yourself the following questions. If you can't answer each well then you may need to reconsider what you are planning to preach.

- What felt need are you trying to address? (Consider the six themes from chapter three.)
- Will this help us live out our why?
- Will people feel inspired?
- Will people feel challenged?
- Is it good news?

Our Plan

Now that you know it is time to act. How will you put what you have learned into action over the next twelve months?

Month:_____

Month:_____

Month:_____

Month:_____

Month:_____

Month:_____

Month:_____

Month:_____

Month:_____

Month:_____

Month:_____

Month:_____

Month:_____